THE DRUID'S
HANDBOOK

POCKET EDITION

Published from
Mardukite Borsippa HQ, San Luis Valley, Colorado
Founding Church of Mardukite Zuism,
Mardukite Academy & Systemology Society
for religious and educational purposes only.

MERLYN STONE'S LONG-LOST CLASSIC

DRUID HANDBOOK

ANCIENT MAGICK FOR A NEW AGE

by Joshua Free writing as Merlyn Stone
Edited and Introduced by Rowen Gardner

THE JOSHUA FREE IMPRINT
JFI PUBLICATIONS

© 2022, JOSHUA FREE

ISBN : 979-8-9864379-6-5

A special pocket version of
The Druid's Handbook

Pocket Paperback Edition — *July 2022*

Also available in hardcover as "Druid's Handbook"
and in "Merlyn's Complete Book of Druidism"

mardukite.com

A _Classic_ of 20th Century Druidology

Come venture into the deepest folds of the Green World... Enter the Sacred Grove and initiate yourself to the greatest Celtic Mystery Tradition ever – The Wisdom of the Druids! Discovering the true Druidic wisdom of these ancient legendary woodland mystics has never been clearer for our times!

Drawing upon over two decades experience in the neodruidic community, the original underground masterpiece by Joshua Free returns to life in this pocket paperback version of the newly revised and expanded 20th anniversary presentation.

Providing a new vision with unparalleled clarity for modern Druidry, world renown occultist and mystic, Joshua Free, explores the magic and deep teachings of Druidic Lore, including core doctrines and codes, triad teachings of the Bards, natural philosophy, the construction of ritual tools and performance of ceremonial magic involving the elements, trees and forces of Nature – all of which is presented in honor of the true spirit of authentic Druidism.

Whether you are new to Druidry or simply looking to refresh your own practices, this concise, expertly written and beautifully presented guide to the ancient mysteries is sure to re-enchant you everyday life with the Wisdom of the Druids!

Pocket Editions Available (as of 2022):
The Druid's Handbook
The Witch's Handbook
Anunnaki Bible – The Cuneiform Scriptures
Anunnaki Rites – The Maqlu Ritual Book
Anunnaki Gods – The Sumerian Religion

TABLET OF CONTENTS

TABLE OF CONTENTS

I. ORGANIZED RELIGION vs. CHRISTIANITY

II. APPENDIX

20TH ANNIVERSARY EDITION
OF 'THE DRUID'S HANDBOOK'

Foreword by Rowen Gardner

AUTHENTIC DRUIDISM! Come venture into the deepest folds of the Green World, enter the Sacred Grove and initiate yourself to the greatest Celtic Mystery Tradition—the Wisdom of the Druids! Discovering true Druidic wisdom of these ancient legendary woodland mystics has never been clearer for our times!

Drawing upon over two decades experience in the neodruidic community, Joshua Free's original underground masterpiece returns to life, newly revised and expanded for this amazing 20th Anniversary presentation. Joshua Free's *"Druid's Handbook"* is a superior addition to any modern Druid's library—as part of a planned reissue of the author's classic trilogy of materials, including *"Draconomicon"* and *"Book of Elven-Faerie."*

Providing a new vision with unparalleled clarity for modern Druidry, world renown occultist and mystic, Joshua Free explores the magic and deep teachings of Druidic Lore, including core doctrines and codes, triad teachings of the Bards, natural philosophy, the construction of ritual tools and performance of ceremonial magic involving trees and Nature—all of which is presented in honor of the true spirit of authentic Druidism.

Whether you are new to Druidry or simply looking to refresh your own practices, this concise, expertly written and beautifully presented guide to the ancient mysteries is sure to re-enchant your everyday life with the *Wisdom of the Druids*.

Druidism is, first and foremost, the "Craft of the Wise," a pure and ancient stream of magic and lore linked directly to the roots of human civilization. What we observe as "Druidry" is simply one manifestation of an undefiled pursuit toward the "Universal Truth" that we all instinctively know exists. The true and authentic Druidic path may be found, in part, at the foundation of all "branches" grown from the original "Ancient Mystery School"—a stream of knowledge and wisdom that surpasses cultural language and semantics of any specific geography or period in history. The author has chosen, for this book, to represent a "branch" of ancient "Western European" esoterica referred to as "Druidism."

Since the inception of the printing press, more ink has been spilled on speculation and intrigue of the Druid Way then any other single ancient cabal of esoteric mystics in history. It is from these same ancient remnants of mysticism, enchantment and natural philosophy that other more familiarly popularized "branches of the arcane tree" have matur-

maturely bloomed for the "New Age." Although modern day occult initiates may be more likely to receive a kaleidoscope of classical images of Egyptian and Mediterranean cultures, deeper research would reveal that "secret societies" of Druids appear behind original lodges and orders of "Freemasonry," "Rosicrucians" and even the "Hermetic Order of the Golden Dawn," not to mention frequent exploitations of the same for the accessible "poor-man" versions of "neopaganism" and "Wicca" that have saturated the "New Age" since the 1970's.

True elements of Druidic Tradition extend beyond the records of simple spells and sadistic sorceries recovered from at least two thousand years of literary material. It is especially during the period of the "Dark Ages"—when the surface world was plummeted into Darkness, following tyrannical reign of the Roman Church—that we experienced a rise in the "magicus ridiculous," or grimoires dedicated to diabolical fantasy in the name of "power," but which offer none but the lowest forms of adrenaline and delusions of grandeur. The wisdom of the Druids surpasses trivial and trite compulsions of human fancy. Its power does not lend itself so easily to corruption as other vehicles that many of today's misinformed seekers are more likely to drive—and these other esoteric car salesman have had a long run of getting people to buy into their snake-oil.

Contrasting a secular world of neodruid debates, Joshua Free's "Druid's Handbook" provides a refreshing breath of new life into an otherwise obscure domain shrouded in mystery and misconception. His presentation of the Druid Legacy clearly establishes its relevance in history—as a significant contributor of traditions, magic, folklore and cultural development all across the Earth, and not only restricted to a localized region of Western Europe that we are quickest to identify as "Celtic."

The beautiful relay of Druidic wisdom contained within these pages is presented without the author succumbing to a stigma of controversy and mudslinging inherent in neodruidic politics—aspects that the author and his esoteric affiliations are no stranger to, but of which lend nothing positive to true seekers of the amazing natural and universal Druid experience. There are too many organizations and supposed "authorities" shedding their own hostile attitudes on their students—leaving the true abilities of discernment out of reach and subject only to some centralized indoctrinated standard—the same ideals that these supposedly "open-minded" folk have sought to escape from the contemporary world by selecting alternative paths in which to invest their energies and base their lives.

In the first underground *Mardukite* release of this

volume—as the title *"Druidry"*—a *Mardukite Alumni*, James Thomas, gives a personal narrative illustrating this experience in his Prologue for that edition:—

> I recognized early on that the Druid Path is a very individual personal quest for enlightenment and also that those that choose to follow and practice this path each carry their own interpretation of it. Personally, I have worked to learn from as many Druidic perspectives and groups as possible, taking a bit with me from each teaching and lesson—admittedly, though, I have always felt the strongest *pull* toward Douglas Monroe and his "Merlyn" books, ultimately "Pheryllt Druidry" in general. This *pull* has come with receiving my share of grief from the supposed "real Druids" who apparently know everything about the ancients and feel they are able to judge all branches and flavors of modern-day Druidry, *because...?* Well, I've never really found an answer to this question... They feel *threatened?* Or, maybe it's pure *ignorance?* Whatever the case, I started to not even view these kinds of people as "real Druids" at all. *Real Druids* do not maliciously attack others for their teachings...

Joshua Free's "Druid's Handbook" reflects a <u>holistic</u> approach to the "Druid Way," a *"systemology"* that is uniquely present in all works by the author—and to which I am privileged the opportunity to add "more light" to it for this edition. In many ways, and in spite of its ongoing evolution throughout its author's lifetime, the work is deserving of "more light." Genuine power inherent in the author's writings comes from a place in Self that most readers used to contemporary "New Age" puff-ball materials are at risk to overlook. The true teachings of authentic Druidism are drawn from the supreme teacher of its mysteries—Nature—and these are so simple in their mathematical precision that they are easily dismissed, just as equally is the case concerning other tomes and volumes presented by Joshua Free, ever since the original 1990's underground appearance of *"Draconomicon,"* *"Sorcerer's Handbook"* and *"Druid's Bible"* while writing under the name "Merlyn Stone."

Where many other books on "druidism" have appeared in the New Age marketplace, what we actually find is either a synthesis of various aspects of Celtic mythology, or else a revised tradition of established ritual magic or "wiccan" elements that simply incorporate Celtic themes. *"The Druid's Handbook"* was written for personal use—privately circulated to members of the author's own networks—then later released to the under ground under a pseudonym—"Merlyn Stone"—the name the author operated with from 1995 until 2005, mainly lending it to "Druidic" publications, such as the "*Draconomicon*" and "*Sorcerer's Handbook,*" prior to publicly developing his current "Mardukite Research Organization."

I introduce the work by Joshua Free as "authentic Druidism" fully aware of how controversial that phrase is to so many of the critics who will read these words. But—it *is* authentic, in that it presents an undefiled pursuit of Truth, and in the spirit of the famous Druid's motto: *Truth against the world* —else the pursuit of Truth *against all odds* and *overcoming all adversity.* It is, by its very nature, a personal exploration into the *root of all things* and the *mysteries of the universe*—and we can look to no other authorities for our answers, only gentle guidance. This guidance, I believe, is very present in this book—and the *Self-Honest* experience of this guidance is what I believe constitutes a justified endorsement of these lessons as "authentic." Only the *Seeker* can determine if this is the case for themselves—no one else can provide this discernment; no one else is responsible for your *Self-actualization.*

It is the *Self-honest*, unfiltered and untainted, pursuit of the highest Truth that distinguishes the Druid Way from so many other potential avenues of discovery. Many are called into the folds of its

"Universalist Tradition" for that reason alone—and we also find that it is a highly analytical, intellectual and studious path to tread as well. Prior to the author's choice of the phrase "*Self-Honesty*" to reflect an unadulterated experience of reality, the Druids simply called the same state: "Truth." And we could continue to use this word as an absolute today were it not for the degradation of its meaning—for we are no longer taught to pursue this "Truth" in our world today. Our surface world thrives only on mediocrity, falling in step, and believing what former generations of "seekers" have dictated as reality.

In a previous version of these materials—released publicly as "*The Book of Druidry*" by Joshua Free —dauntless street mystic, Breanna "Maxine" Bender, offers a similar sentiment in her Foreword to that edition:—

> In the World distinguishing the Druids, nothing more asserted their Honor than their duty to Truth—and this Truth inspired extraordinary methods of inquiry, discerning questions and answers through one's own *individuality* without illusion. And one of the few first things I absorbed from what the ancient Druid's taught was learning to accept truth and trust my own intuition, especially when I wanted to follow my curiosities and inclinations.

The Druids also taught how essential Memory was to our survival—that you couldn't know who you are or where you're going if you didn't remember the Truth about who and what you were and where you came from. For example, Druids believed in transmigration, otherwise known as reincarnation. This means we have experienced being born, being alive and a physical death many times before—although our soul stays eternal.

In Nature—and all throughout the dimension we exist in—all things, all there is in existence, is interrelated with everything else. And the Druid believed that we are also connected to this *everythingness*—that we already know everything; we only but need to remember what we have forgotten. This demonstrates how complex we are as an Identity, celebrating our uniqueness. Without your special presence manifesting itself into History, this Reality would not manifest the way it is today. So many channels of energy are constantly clashing and colliding into and onto itself that eventually ordinary space is required to manifest a transmutation of the chaos into something unique. And consequently, everything in existence carries its own vibration that manifests in our reality of space...

No longer restricted to antiquarian fraternities and "secret societies," a pursuit for "Druid wisdom" that captivated several successive generations has fallen upon the modern and NexGen *Seekers*— those who have chosen, or rather *been chosen*, to take up the cause and maintain the undying integrity of the Druid Way—for there are *always* "Druids" *somewhere* on Earth.

There is an immortal timeless Druid presence on the planet—one that surpasses any clinical definition of "Druidism." It is the *definition* and *classification* of what "Druidism" means that modern "neodruids" are most likely to debate: *this* is or is not "Celtic"; *that* is not from a "true Druidic" source; *this* author is not of British descent; *that* ritual suggestion is not from the right European time period—all of this keeps the uninitiated from gaining a true and faithful Druid experience: which, by definition, involves the spiritual and intellectual discernment of whatever they cross paths with on their own. Without this key feature, no real wisdom is achieved; only blind faith.

As defining "Druidism" is no easy feat, it is most appropriate to prime the reader of this current book with a clear definition provided by the author himself—from the Introduction to a recently released anthology edition of his "*Book of Pheryllt*" recension as "*Draconomicon, Vol. 2: The Pheryllt Researches*":—

In ancient Keltia, the Druid Order consisted of learned ones, those educated in Bardic Arts: cosmology and spirituality, natural-native history and geology, legendary history of heroes and mythology, healing and botanical medicine, astronomy and astrology, and of course *magic*—all of which are hidden in lines of Bardic verse and the researches of those who study them. As primary preservers of Celtic and Druid Mysteries, it is no wonder that Bardic Druids were considered the transmitter or catalyst of -*awen*- the essence, Divine Spark or spirit of inspiration that the Greeks termed *gnosis*. It is to the "ebb and flow" of the -*awen field*- that the magical and poetic genius of the Bard is attributed.

Preservation of ancient knowledge is key among all elite orders of the ages. This Ancient Mystery School is timeless and spans all places on Earth. Past mystical cultures often relied on elite orders of scribe-priests and poet-magicians to bridge ancestral roots and traditions with the future—orders rooted in *languages*, *communication*, and above all the written word. The poetic genius of *awen*—an eternal Divine Spark of Creation—manifests throughout all creative arts and as the spirit of "prophecy," an ability to observe all reality experiences with a heightened awareness and communicate it in the World of Form.

Druidism is, therefore, an echo of this "poetic genius," an amalgamation of collected knowledge preserved by the ancient elite, including a mystical and scientific understanding of the world that eluded the perceptual range of the larger "common" population.

I have watched as Joshua Free's efforts and aptitude has continued to soar over the course of a quarter-of-a-century, and I do believe Douglas Monroe said it best in his preface to Free's recension of *Pheryllt* or *Draconomicon, Volume 2*:—

I have watched as Joshua has matured into a fine writer—an even better scholar—and in my opinion, Joshua's genius lies in his ability to compile, categorize and connect vast stockpiles, ancient to modern, and which has, over the past decade, culminated in a truly impressive contribution to world metaphysics. In time, I believe his work will receive more of the serious recognition it deserves.

It is my hope that the time for appreciating his collected work will arrive—sooner, rather than later —for all those who are called to find resonance with the ineffable Truth.

...And may that Truth set you free!

Wishing you the best from the arms of the Dragon.

—Rowen Gardner
Summer 2019
rev. Summer 2022
Wales, U.K.

INTRODUCTION TO
'THE DRUID'S HANDBOOK'

by Joshua Free

Twenty-five years have now passed since I first became active in modern Druidism. My original debut underground publication—known as *Draconomicon*—resulted from research notebooks I kept during that period—and another, more widely circulated volume—the *Sorcerer's Handbook*—developed from a completely separate collection of notes. These early writings from the 1990's—under the pseudonym of "Merlyn Stone"—sealed my fate for participation in the "New Age" occult underground. It led me on an incredible journey that has since included an inception of the "Mardukite Research Organization" and "NexGen Systemological Society."

These later groups emerged immediately following my first two new-millennium underground publications—*Book of Elven-Faerie* and *Arcanum: The Great Magical Arcanum*. Few are aware, however, that between these two periods of writing, I had completed another manuscript—after *Draconomicon* and *Sorcerer's Handbook*, but before *Book of Elven-Faerie*—that most strongly encapsulated the spirit of what some might consider "traditional Druidism" than any of my other more esoteric or controversial literary contributions. My exploratins into the core fundamental Druid *systemology* led to its original working title: "Applied Druidology," but of which is now presented to you in commemoration of its 20th Anniversary as "The Druid's Handbook."

It is a joy, after so many years, to see a newer, expanded and greatly improved version of "The Druid's Handbook" that exceeds the abilities I possessed as an underground researcher and publisher a quarter-of-a-century ago. The world is also a different place—far and removed from New Age peaks and breakthroughs taking place in the mid-1990's when "underground esoterica" started becoming more publicly visible.

We suddenly saw a huge revival in "magickal" interests swell from its incline in the 1970's and 1980's as the "New Age marketplace" first formed. Suddenly these obscure oddities once reserved to dark alleys and dank fens now started to grace the shopping centers and local malls. More titles were flooding into "New Age" and "supernatural/paranormal" genres than ever before. Publishers were quick to find anyone that would lend their personal spellbooks and Books of Shadows to the market. Suddenly being in a "coven" was fashionable, and we were overrun with a significant amount of repetitive "neopagan" materials all validating each other within hermetically sealed confines of this new "movement." Most of these fell by the wayside; a few became underground cult classics—but in my opinion, little advancement has since been made in the mainstream/contemporary New Age approaches, and in fact, most newer rehashes have become quite diluted when compared to their former source texts.

While the mainstream has remained mostly fixed on neopagan ideologies that often revive any or all aspects of ancient pantheism and cultural mythologies arbitrarily—we have seen an increase in progressive activity in the underground, also publicly visible during the new millennium, particularly related to the rising use of the internet and especially the "Web 2.0" that quickly resulted, far more interactive and focused on social networking than the static internet of the 1990's. While it did open up many "underground" elements and facets of lore to the public, it also greatly enabled those of us already working in the underground to develop covert networks and alliances as a reaction—or perhaps antidote—to rapid world changes. Sometimes these alliances grew less covert over time, particularly in regard to "independent publishing," which is the only surface-world industry that actively feeds our type of work. It hits those of us who have had much to say, but for whatever the reasons, have been slighted out by the "big game" players and are usually forced to remain in the underground suppo ted by small followings. And it is not a matter of merit. There is a lot of politics at play—even in an "enlightening New Age."

The Druid Path is a continuous realization of discovery and it never truly ends in this lifetime. Graduation equals "Ascension" and this is the road we are journeying on—moving ever closer to Wholeness: the *unifying oneness* of the Cosmos; the beautiful harmony of Cosmic Law reflected everywhere in Nature; and gaining total awareness of our participation with Reality throughout what we call "existence." "Mysteries of the Druids" are not simply *learned*; they are *lived* and *experienced*. This is the only way true knowledge matures into wisdom.

"Druid's Handbook" is an integral part of a literary serial that relays my presentation of Druidic Tradition for the 21st Century. Our current volume focuses on underlying systemology of both ancient and modern Druid methods of philosophy and learning. This unique background compliments other titles in this series trilogy including the "Draconomicon" and "Book of Elven-Faerie." The goal then is not to repeat information from each title— rather it is to extend an examination of the Druid Legacy from three angles or sides so as to provide the best and most wide-angle treatment of the subject. They are each quite unique on their own—but they also contribute to a large all-encompassing self-initiation program offering an unparalleled understanding of the ancient Druid Mystery Tradition for the new millennium.

A critical history concerning development of Danubian Druids and Welsh Druidism among ancient Celts, in addition to many practices revived for contemporary "New Age" traditions—including core rituals dedicated to the elements and trees —all appears in the volume documenting Druidry from the angle of the "Elven-Faerie Way."

Complimenting this, another volume is dedicated to examining a prehistoric "Dragon Legacy" that emerged from the most ancient world of the cradle of civilization that was left in the wake of evolving Druidism, beneath the surface of all developing Eurasian traditions, as lore and wisdom of the Ancient Mystery School radiated outward from its remote and legendary esoteric sources. Our *current volume* seeks to bridge these other works with a fundamental core!

"The Druid's Handbook" is then an archive of lessons that may be used by themselves to relay the beautiful simplistic natural harmony of the "Druid Way"—or they may be used to provide the same as a structure for further, deeper, investigations into the Druid Mystery Tradition, provided in the collective series. As a combination of materials, the work provides the most universal and complete synthesis available to modern *Seekers*—those that have few solid avenues to turn to for contemporary instruction and true apprenticeship in the 21st century.

This volume relays a concise examination of core facets pertaining to the Druid Way that allows a *Seeker* to glean deeper levels of emotional, intellectual and spiritual knowledge (and abilities of awareness) than some more "colorful" presentations provide—those emphasizing iconic symbolism towards, for example, the "Elven-Faerie Way" or "Dragon Path." Those uninitiated to deeper levels of understanding may misappropriate the *cosmic code* that underlies these other "angles." But, *All-is-One*—ALL is connected and there is nothing existing that exists in exclusion to everything else. This means that hidden within the folds of time, space and all the cosmic magic holding it together, we discover this ancient current returning to the Source of All Being and Creation— little known, popularly referenced, mostly misunderstood—a facet of history closely influencing evolution of all Western traditions and cultures: the DRUIDS.

Beyond simple—not always inaccurate— stereotypes of white-robed priestly men gathering in stone circles near oak groves, the Druid Tradition is laden with a much deeper philosophy of living spiritual mysticism. It is still quite available to us —and in such intensity, power and brightly woven colors, that we see no richer equal developed in the history of Western culture. And in many respects, the bring array of *Celtic* lore has most certainly attracted its share of attention—but there are many challenges remaining for modern *Seekers* in search of truly worthy resources to base a pursuit of the *Druid Way*. It is my hope that the reader will find this book to be one of those.

As is greatly needed for our world and our times—and of which has been known to a select few in the world at all times—the map to find the pure stream of Druidic philosophy and spirituality can be revealed in the most simple language; as it has always been and is intended to be: relayed privately in the forests, woodlands and wilds of the ancient world.

With the shift in our global consciousness-paradigm, coinciding with what many call the "New Age," various alternative methodologies have sprung back into public view—including many facets that lay dormant for centuries, if not millennium. The "New Age" includes revivals of virtually every possible indigenous and pre-Christian source accessible to the inquiry of modern minds during the "information age." Therefore, we should not be surprised to see "Druidism," or any other Celtic niches, making a "come-back" during these times—when the Earth Planet could most surely benefit from additional Druidic Earth Guardians carrying a torch of "ecological responsibility" meaning the "ability to respond" to our ecological crisis—an ecosystem that carries not only physical ramifications, but widespread inescapable emotional, psychological and spiritual ones as well.

We cannot run from this. We cannot expect flawed methods to achieve success on other planets. If we cannot resolve life on this planet, we will never sustain it elsewhere—our physical and spiritual existence, our entire being that seeks to ascend the ladder of cosmic evolution, will be forced to succumb and withdraw in lieu of external transhuman faculties. And these will never truly elevate our *spirit* or *soul*—our "I"—our *Self*. Many of us today believe that *Druidism* is the solution: a cure for what ails the planet and a critical rung on the ladder of our unfolding Ascension... and *you* just might discover this also!

The Truth against the World!

—Joshua Free
Summer 2019

THE DRUID'S HANDBOOK

DRUIDISM AND DRUIDRY

The quest for Druidic Wisdom is not restricted to a specific locale—some small island in Western Europe—or even to a special lineage or bloodline. It is accessible in all places and at all times, making Druidism and Druidry a unique pathway to recognize universal knowledge found everywhere in Nature. Keys to the Druid Way may be discovered without visits to certain buildings, paying homage to obscure gods, or seeking any administration of Truth from arbitrary authorities—for *there is no religion higher than Truth* and there is *no man greater then Truth*. It is the "mystery" of Universal Truth—and the holistic Universal Bond that systematically ties all existence together—that a Druid seeks to unlock on their pathway to Ascension.

Historians, critics and scholars seldom find agreement concerning the traditions or origins of the Druids—of course, the same could be said in regards to the Egyptians and Sumerians. In our present case—the Druids—decoding the mystery is not altogether difficult giving the wide range of new data emerging to connect ancient Druids and their legacy in Europe to distant Mediterranean and Mesopotamian origins. For years this has been a matter of theory, put forth in other volumes within this series, one that has not proved popular throughout the greater "New Age" community, but of which I have relentlessly advocated. The premise—which served as a main tenet for *Book of Elven-Faerie*—is summarized best in Rowen Gardner's foreword to a newly released 25th Anniversary edition of the *Draconomicon:*—

One theory put forth by Joshua Free, and keystone to his writings, regards a prehistoric collective migration of a unique Mesopotamian systemology across Europe, citing examples of the *La Tene* culture and marked by indigenous traditions developing later in vicinity to the Danube River, one of two pathways he suggested that it probably traveled. He states that it is only the result of Roman intervention and the domination of the "Classical World" over the former ancient one that pushed these traditions and evidence for them into specific concentrated locations—such as easily seen today with the "Celtic World" traditionally attributed exclusively to the British Isles or Ireland, yet it once served as a dominating influence for most of the European continent. How easily we forget... One additional facet of his theory is that prior to the migration, a localized concentration of this population emerged from the Ancient Near East and gathered in prehistoric Anatolia—home of the legendary

"Drunemeton"—the secret birthplace of Druidry that only the highest ranks among them knew of and would regularly return to during their lifetimes. All wild theories? In April 2019, the BBC headlines read: "DNA Reveals Origins of Stonehenge Builders." Articles provided research summaries published in *Nature, Ecology & Evolution*. It described a neolithic western migration in c. 6000 B.C. from Anatolia, modern-day Turkey, across two routes—Mediterranean and Danube River Valley—which spread early Mesopotamian knowledge of agriculture across Europe, reaching Britain by c. 4000 B.C...

For many years, the traditional textbook consensus remained that the British Druids were part of a bronze age migration from the mainlands. Other legends of mythic proportion assert that the Druids were survivors of some lost continent or the civilization of Atlantis—making "prehistoric Druidism" at least as old as the "Sumerian Anunnaki" tradition of Mesopotamia—and, if that were true, they might even emerge from similar origins. It is more likely that Druidry, and practice of its high intellectual ideals, were *exported to* Western Europe separate from the indigenous traditions of prehistoric Celts.

The obscure ancient nature of the Druids did not

escape the notice of antiquarian scholars, such as
W. Winwood Reade in *"Mysteries of the Druids"*
(*Book III*) where he writes:—

> "Although the term Druid is local, their re-
> ligion was of deep root, and a distant ori-
> gin. It was of equal antiquity with those of
> the Persian Magi, the Chaldees of Assyria,
> and the Brachmans of Hindostan. It re-
> sembled them so closely in its sublime pre-
> cepts, in its consoling promises, as to leave
> no doubt that these nations, living so
> widely apart, were all of the same stock
> and the same religion–that of Noah, and
> the children of men before the flood. They
> worshiped but one God, and erected to him
> altars of earth, or unhewn stone, and
> prayed to him in the open air; and believed
> in a heaven, in a hell, and in the immortal-
> ity of the soul. It is strange that these off-
> spring of the patriarchs should also be cor-
> rupted from the same sources, and should
> thus still preserve a resemblance to one an-
> other in minor tenets of their polluted
> creeds..."

Druid Tradition, as we best know it today, was carried across mainland Europe from the Mesopotamian and Mediterranean regions coinciding with
a cultural dispersion from prehistoric pre-dynastic
periods of Mesopotamia, and perhaps also Egypt,

meaning before 3200 B.C. Prior to this, humans are in a state of constant "awakening" as they learn to establish themselves *again* after the "Deluge" conditions concurrently marking the end of the last Ice Age era.

According to the Irish "*Book of Invasions*," specifically "Celtic" lands, or *Keltia*—Britain/Wales, Ireland, Gaul/France and Scotland, &tc.—were all subject to different races of invaders ever since prehistoric times, and not necessarily restricted to those exclusively "Druidic." What we identify as "Druidry" today is related to the arrival of Western European "Danubian Druidism," carried to the British Isles by way of the La Tene culture that migrated westward across the Danube and Rhine Rivers.

The "*Book of Invasions*" describes several "waves" of invasion and various cycles of political, spiritual and racial change on the isles. The first or oldest record of habitation beginning at the end of the Ice Age is attributed to the Nemedians (or "Sons of the Son"), then the Fomorians ("People of the Sea"), the Fir-Bolg ("Men of Dark Earth") and finally, in the end, the arrival of Danubian Druidism via the Tuatha de Dannan—or, as the current author has suggested, "Tuatha d'Anu"—the "Bright Ones" and "Children of the Stars" ("Children of Anu") that most significantly shaped the face of "Celtic Druidism" as we perceive it today.

It is important for the *Seeker* to keep in mind that the total sum of Druidic Wisdom is of such antiquity and esoteric mystique—in relation to contemporary modern systems—that it is perhaps distantly rooted in some prehistoric or otherwise unknown "civilization"—and as such we must keep an open mind about possible revelations and discoveries that may be yielded with fresh new or clear *Self-Honest* eyes... *To see the world in a grain of sand...*

Egotism, ethnocentrism and any fashion of filter used to sift perception, or experience of knowledge, will always keep the receipt of wisdom from being rooted in true knowledge or understood in "*Self-Honesty*"—the ability to see things for how they really are. Many times over, a person will operate and experience "reality" based on false precepts, and while all things may appear "true," this false validation will hinder awareness of objective Truth.

When presented with ancient wisdom and knowledge—what stems from obscure sources stretching into prehistory—it is sometimes difficult for the "modern psyche" or False-Ego to accept that there is anything relevant to be gleaned from the past. Humanity cannot accept that they live in the shadows of something that has come before—paralleling, perhaps even exceeded, what we "know" today—philosophically, mystically, spiritually, and yes, even technologically.

Druids bridge the "gap" between the long forgotten "yesterday" and the taken-for-granted "today." Their Celtic presence supplied a culture with knowledge, science, religion and tradition—occupying a time in recorded history "after the sky gods had left the earth" and during the rise of "avatars" and "earth deities" fashioned from the lives of "heroes" now dominating our surviving accounts of "Celtic mythology." Some of these accounts were specific to the "Celts" themselves, those native to Europe relating to the arrival of the Tuatha De Dannan (or Tuatha d'Anu), those that carried "Druidism" to the region—the "Dragon Legacy" and remnants of an ancient "Sky God" tradition. When they arrived in Keltia, their higher wisdom and faculties made them seem as "gods" to the more primitive and tribal Celtic people—and "Celtic Druidism" was born.

If we step back for a moment and take the wide angle view, let us consider our knowledge base: arrival of Danubian Druids subsequently led to a unification of nomadic and primitive Celtic tribes under a national "religion," thereby securing a "governing state," a standard held under that "religion" as a means of "domesticating" humanity to advance "the Arts of Civilization" in Europe. *This* is a story that we have actually seen played out before—at the potential birthplace of this tradition, from the "cradle of civilization" in Mesopotamia, when "Anunnaki" high-minds met with more primitive populations, leading to an archetypal blueprint of *systemology*, once specific to traditions dedicated to the Sumerian and Babylonian "Sky Gods," but later influencing the core of all global paradigms, from the Egyptian to the Semitic, from the Druidic to the Judeo-Christian—global Ancient Mystery Schools all shared a common origin and streamline back to the Source.

History is recursive—cycling back onto itself repeatedly—and we gauge our perception of time based on intervals of the same peaks and valleys that our histories have already shown us before. Wisdom comes from clear observation, and it would be no coincidence that the "priests" of these traditions are, in fact, "lore-masters" and "archivists" of the arcane knowledge.

It is not hard to imagine the awesome spiritual and worldly power of the Druids in ancient Celtic society—their absolute place in that realm sharing no equal for at least a millennium. But, it is by written accounts of the classical period Greeks and Romans that we are "officially" introduced to the Druids in history—potentially thousands of years after the development of these early migratory leaders unbeknownst to rising populations in the Mediterranean and surrounding regions. There were certainly Druids still occupying Turkey, or

Anatolia, during the time of Christ, because we find several letters to them from Paul in the Christian New Testament, addressing them as the "Galatians"—from which the Celtic lands of "Gaul" (now France) were also named for.

Historically, we cannot overlook that the very position of the "Druid" in Celtic society closely mirrored many elements we identify in older documented traditions of Mesopotamia. This is one more aspect to consider when confirming origins and migration of an original unifying ancient esoteric standard. The strong description provided by W. Winwood Reade in "Mysteries of the Druid" succinctly proves that antiquarian scholars were more than familiar with classical descriptions of "Druid Power" exercised in Celtic society:—

> "This priesthood flourished in Gaul and in Britain, and in the islands which encircled them. In whichever country they may first have struck root we at least know that the British Druids were the most famous, and that it was a custom in the time of Julius Cæsar for the Gallic students to cross the British channel to study in the seminaries of the sister island. But by that time, Druidism had begun to wane in Gaul, and to be deprived of many of its privileges by the growing intelligence of the secular power.

"The Druids possessed remarkable powers and immunities. Like the Levites, the Hebrews, and Egyptian priests, they were exempted from taxes and from military service. They also annually elected the magistrates of cities: they educated all children of whatever station, not permitting their parents to receive them till they were fourteen years of age. Thus the Druids were regarded as the real fathers of the people. The Persian Magi were entrusted with the education of their sovereign; but in Britain the kings were not only brought up by the Druids, but also relieved by them of all but the odium and ceremonies of sovereignty.

"These powerful priests formed councils of the state, and declared peace or war as they pleased. The poor slave whom they seated on a throne, and whom they permitted to wear robes more gorgeous even than their own was surrounded, not by his noblemen, but by Druids. He was a prisoner in his court, and his jailors were inexorable, for they were priests. There was a Chief Druid to advise him, a bard to sing to him, a *sennechai*, or chronicler, to register his action in the Greek character, and a physician to attend to his health, and to cure or kill him as the state required.

"All the priests in Britain and all the physicians, all the judges and all the learned men, all the pleaders in courts of law and all the musicians belonged to the order of the Druids. It can easily be conceived then that their power was not only vast but absolute. In all things, therefore, they endeavored to draw a line between themselves and the mass. In their habits, in their demeanor, in their very dress. They wore long robes which descended to the heel, while that of others came only to the knee; their hair was short and their beards long, while the Britons wore but mustaches on their upper lips, and their hair generally long. Instead of sandals they wore wooden shoes of a pentagonal shape, and carried in their hands a white wand called *slatan drui'eachd*, or magic wand, and certain mystical ornaments around their necks and upon their breasts..."

Approaching mysteries of Druidic Wisdom today —with modern eyes and using only classical accounts by cultures *outside* the system being described—can certainly be a daunting task. Our contemporary culture today operates under a different premise—one ruled by capitalism and external technologies—and so, many facets of ancient wisdom and the magical traditions revived in the "New Age" seem outlandish or incorrectly interpreted for our times and our future. Society no longer celebrates its "philosophers" or "high thinkers" except when the product of their vision is immediately proprietary and marketable. We seem to value little else, and certainly none of the spiritual faculties and "internal technologies" we have at our disposal to develop—those that actually empower the *Self* and accelerate it toward *true* "transhuman" Ascension.

Those past civilizations dependent primarily on their outward "external" technologies and infrastructure in order to survive generally fall every time. We do not see this faculty in Nature, which operates on its own evolutionary tract of programming. With humanity, however, there is a constant "imbalance"—most likely due to its evolutionary upgrading by outside influences. This *does* separate us—on an apparent level—from our naturally evolving environment, and as such humans are held to a greater degree of "responsibility" or "ability to respond" that we often equate with "power." But, in order to achieve our goals of true spiritual Ascension to a higher existence, we must unite outer achievements with internal advancement; whether we choose to call it "spiritual" or "consciousness" or "magic," is a personal semantic choice.

BRINGING DRUIDISM TO LIFE

True wisdom and philosophies of the ancient Druids are not demonstrated in *exoteric* academia or the public history books that are most accessible. The current author's choice to differentiate previous academic pursuits into classical sources and stereotypes with a newly invigorated field of "*Esoteric Druidology*" is reflected in this current volume.

Ideals of the human condition have never changed. We seek to achieve a certain view of "perfection" today just as ancient Druids believed that all life moved along a steady progression back to the pure Source from which it emerged. That being said— our vision has changed. Society believes our immortality or "Ascension" is only to be achieved "externally," using only "external technologies" to extend lifetimes, increase flows of information and attempt "outer space" colonization. But, it is our living conditions—what it is to be *human*—that must be elevated, coupled with internal skills of heightened receptivity to the "reality" we experience, in order to properly evolve. We have been given an accelerated fast track in our genetics that is simply waiting to be unfolded.

Throughout history, Druidism represents the individual pursuit of Truth by living the "Right Way," in harmony with the Natural world, reaching toward a Self-Honest "equilibrium" between the *Self* and the *Universe* until we live the daily experience that the two are *One*. An integration of such knowledge into modern living philosophies seems *esoteric* or counter-cultural—the paradigm does not seem to fit with the "world-at-large," and appears rather rebellious, as the antithesis to its standards. Perhaps that is just what our world needs to fend off its charted course toward annihilation.

Druidism is eternal, a timeless pursuit of Truth in accordance with Cosmic Law—or Natural Law—that is reflected in the acts and equations of some group or secret cabal in some place at every point in history. As a result, the academic world is not always able adequately "date" or "allocate" all aspects of the ancient world as they truly are. Most branches of archaeology are rooted in assumptions that later research takes for granted, thereby propagating them as facts and often adjusting the more recent findings or assumptions to corroborate previous ones. It is only within the current millennium that we witness a strong ratification of previous held beliefs in every field of science and learning cultivated during the 20th century.

Our modern understanding of Druidism is mainly restricted to what is classifiable as "Celtic Druidism"—but it is very important that we do not confuse these terms. They are conjoined so often that it is easy to blur what distinguishes them—and it is clear that what the words "Celtic" and "Druid" socially mean to us even changes over time. The words themselves, as we identify them in literature, are of Greek origin—appearing to us as *keltoi* and *drui*—from classical accounts of cross-cultural encounter. In Britain, the (Welsh) term "*Derwydd*" applied exclusively to members initiated to the highest order within the "Bardic Colleges" of Druidic instruction.

The first point of distinction: the term "Celtic" is cultural, and applies to certain European races, their national lands and, of course, the colorful heritages attached. By definition, "Druids" represented a class of "learned" and "educated" individuals demonstrating unique aptitude in any particular aspect of the sciences or "Arts of Civilization." This class of "wise ones" is beyond any specific cultural semantic or locale and certainly not restricted to any one interpretation or language. It is very much the case that the same class of individuals, linked to the same Ancient Mystery School, existed simultaneously in other Eurasian and Near-Eastern cultures, known by other "titles" and even within the same Celtic regions before the classical age. Thus, Druidism is not strictly related to Celtic subjects.

We do find slight evidence in arcane literary materials that allude to prehistoric pre-Druidic, or rather "proto-Druidic" lore of a legendary "Pheryllt" group established in Welsh mountains of Snowdonia by c. 3200 B.C. It is difficult to ascertain if this group is related to the later arrival of the Tuatha de Dannan ("Tuatha d'Anu") or Danubian Druids. We cannot rule out that the two may have shared a common origin. Regardless, a prehistoric amalgamation of these minds resulted into what we later refer to as "Druidism." Semantically neither group originally used this title to represent themselves, nor do we academically classify them as "Druids" in history. This further leads to inhibited understanding of Druidic mysteries and enshrouds the subject with additional layers of mystique.

Studies regarding the direct cultural contributions offered by these two proto-Druidic groups are explored at length in two other volumes within this current series—*Draconomicon* and *Book of Elven-Faerie*. A few critical facets from these volumes may lend additional context to the body of knowledge presented in the *Druid's Handbook*.

Lore suggests that the "Children of the Stars" arrived in Keltia on "Beltane"—May's Eve—approximately five thousand years ago. The race or clan was socially represented by four primary "leaders" or "warriors," each from a different city or capital in their "homelands"—wherever this might be, as the subject turns to the domain of legend. Each of the four cities, and the leaders respectively, carried an alignment or affinity with one of the four fundamental elements of Nature— Earth, Air, Fire and Water—and each brought with them a specific artifact or "magical implement" corresponding with that element. This lore provided basis for elemental tools and correspondences in Druidic Tradition.

```
Earth – North – Stone of Fal
Air – East – Spear of Lugh
Fire – South – Sword of Nuada
Water – West – Cauldron of Dagda
```

It is easy to see how these "Gifts of Faerie"—as they are often called in lore—became the very basis for magical implements and tools. For example, the transference of the "air-spear" to an "air-wand" in ritual and ceremonial "magick." Some traditions still refer to these ritual tools as "elemental weapons," and after examining these ancient sources of knowledge, it is clear as to why.

The legacy of the Tuatha de Dannan (Tuatha d'Anu) survived directly in the beliefs and traditions of the native Celts. Many of the names appearing in early "Celtic mythology"—those referred to as "gods" and "goddesses" in "Celtic religion"—are drawn from the histories and memories of Danubian Druids themselves—their leaders, warriors and magicians. They are not represented in the religion as "Celestials" or "Sky Gods," and are instead "earth deities," perhaps descendents of the former—but very physical and very "mortal." These men of and women of renown were distinguished from the common populations—revered for their phenomenal abilities, power, knowledge and/or wisdom. Later, Druids participated in this same tradition and were considered as like a "separate race" among the Celts. They were not "gods" in the same sense of the word in Mesopotamia or Egypt, but they possessed knowledge as if they "came from the stars," and initiated select members of each generation to this Ancient Mystery School.

Druids maintained nearly a millennium of peace in *Keltia* before the first hostile encounters with the Romans. The Druid Order, as a "fraternity," operated alongside an equally significant "sorority" called the Motherhood—or Sisterhood—of "Avalon" (now called Glastonbury Tor). Both of these organizations heavily influenced perceptions of European Magicians, Wizards and Witches as social archetypes. The idea of gender-separated "Mystery Schools" is not unique to Druidic Tradition alone. We can recognize it strongly in Mesopotamia too, where Priests of Nabu and Marduk operated separate schools and temples from the Priestesses of Sarpanit, Inanna-Ishtar or Teshmet. There were also times when both worked together.

Unlike more "politically correct" interpretations of mixed-gender traditions in modern Wicca and/or neopaganism, the methodology of Druid Tradition more correctly reflects membership in "Freemasonry," divided equally between a "Blue Lodge" for the males, and the "Order of Eastern Star" for the females—the "Eastern Star" being, of course, *Venus*, the archetypal planetary embodiment of all chief "goddesses."

Ancient Druids observed the natural Cosmic Law of gender-polarity in all creation and their methods of instruction. Males were given instruction based on a "solar path" oriented to the air and fire elements—and their esoteric correspondences. Females played an equal role in Celtic society, yet aside from key events, ceremonies and festivals, their initiation and instruction took place remotely from male Druids. Their "lunar path" was also distinctly aligned to the water and earth elements, with a stronger emphasis on feminine "goddess" archetypes. Although now a point of contention in today's LGBTQ+ world, the original tradition was observed exactly as described.

Encounters between Celtic Druids and the classical world of Greeks began in c. 800 B.C., and it is from these other literary accounts that our academic definitions of "Druidism" takes shape. Our history books most frequently cite Roman compilations, set down little more than 2,000 years ago by an empire that sought to destroy all traces of true Druidry. These Roman accounts concerning Celts, Druids, and their "religion," were politically biased and even rooted in religious classifications that the Romans could relate to their own "religion," and not as the Celtic people actually experienced it. As a result, these academic accounts completely misrepresent and misinterpret cultural beliefs and traditions of the Celts and Druids.

Many classical renderings pertaining to the Druids by foreign hands are contradictory. What's worse —in the case of the Romans—many writings are meant as propaganda to justify and fuel the *Gaulish Wars* and conquests of the Celtic lands and its people by the Roman Empire—which sought to reign supreme over the entire "known world." Consequently, the Roman accounts tend to be more "brutal" than the few obscure Greek ones. Romans painted a picture of the Celts as little more than ignorant savages obsessed with human gore and naïve Nature "worship." Yet, the Romans must have covertly held Druids in high regard, because they were afraid of their "magic" and spent more resources and time—nearly a millennium— trying to eradicate it, than any other "enemy" they encountered. But sadly, it is these same biased foreign accounts of the Druids that our modern historians and academicians have mainly relied upon to understand Druidism, Druidry and its wisdom.

Romans suppressed the practice of Druidry by force for nearly one thousand years—first independently via invasions, then with the *Gaulish Wars* and finally by uniting their empire with the "Church." In effect, this last move actually plunged the entire Western world into the "Dark Ages." By the year 100 B.C., the Romans pushed most remaining vestiges of Druidry out of Gaul (France) and into Britain. Then they invaded Britain—forcing the last Druids to seek sanctuary in Ireland, the place of their last publicly known refuge. Before it was able to conquer Ireland, the Roman Empire fell—but the damage had been done, and their militant withdrawal from *Keltia* did little to resolve what was lost, leaving the lands and its people in a state of vulnerability when a new brand of Roman empire arrives to conquer the world: The Church of Rome.

With rising Celtic conversion to Christianity, any practice of Druidism was forced to take on a form of passive resistance to disguise its presence—such as in the instance of the "*Culdee,*" an early sect of Celtic Christianity that has almost passed into the realm of legend. It retained much of the original beauty accessed in Gnostic traditions of Christianity later flushed out for officially canonized "Catholic" versions.

But, when Saint Patrick visited Ireland in 432 A.D., he consecrated the land to the Roman

54

Church and forced the last of the 'snakes' from the isle, marking the end of public Druidism. In 563 A.D. Avalon fell to Christian hands and reformed as "Glastonbury Abbey."

REVITALIZING THE SPIRIT OF DRUIDRY

In our previous chapters we have illuminated the physical or historical aspect of "Druidism"—meaning the study of ancient Druidic Tradition, or even modern practices, at an academic or intellectual level. For many, the idea of practical "Druidry" in our current age is ridiculous, following an assumption that there are no clear publicly visible historical records worthy of basing a modern tradition of actual Druidic practices or a revival of its philosophical and spiritual facets.

Classical accounts—particularly those by the Romans—would have us believe that the Druids were practically illiterate, never committing any of their teachings to writing. If true, we would assume that it should not have required a millennium to annihilate their legacy. We know from their own national exchanges and those with other cultures—such as the Greeks—that the Druids were anything but illiterate and prized preservation of true knowledge over all other worldly pursuits.

Systematic apprenticeship and personal initiation to Druidic Tradition did pass verbally through an individualized program developed by a teacher for their student—but this could not be the sole means of retaining Druidic Wisdom. If we consider how great of a reach the Druid Order possessed across Europe, than it would certainly make sense that these intellectuals would value memorization, distributing knowledge lessons in mnemonic flavors —but centralized storehouses of knowledge also existed, mostly hidden away from populated areas. Close examination will reveal the Romans misrepresented this too, for they tell us that the "Druids wrote nothing down," yet also disguised references alluding to the destruction of Druidic libraries—burning both them and the tree groves surrounding them. Hundreds of these allegedly nonexistent libraries disappeared. The Romans were quite thorough in their millennium of malice, seeking under every rock and behind every tree in their efforts to eradicate all traces of Druidic Wisdom.

Some of these Druid libraries kept records in non-traditional ways—even using leaves and other coded writing styles. They were certainly not illiterate, because during the classical era, the Druids used the Greek alphabet in diplomatic correspondence—but they also retained their own secret methods of communication and cryptic runes. As mentioned, they even used the very trees of the sacred groves to preserve their natural philosophy and wisdom as "living forest libraries." We can only imagine the amazing energy vibrated from such a magical environment—lines of leaves strung on cords, stones etched with strange glyphs or shaped into monuments—all of which contributes to our themes of "fantasy" preserved in cultural or genetic memory.

"Strange" "magical" places we often think are only real in our imaginative "fairy tales" *do* actually exist—and at our deepest level, we intuitively all *know* this. At the same time, we have experienced the aftermath of a long period of history known as the "Dark Ages"—or referred to in other related lore as the "Thousand-Year Elven-Faerie Holocaust." It was not until this former era gave way to our "re-enlightenment" period a few hundred years ago, that Druidism and Druidry reemerged into public view. It is quite possible that the sudden return of the "Druid" to global consciousness was a natural and direct response to growing urbanization and rise of industrialization in human society. Even as a modern "secret society" or fraternity, the "neodruidic revival" predates all modern "New Age" movements—including Wicca, schools of Theosophy and even the Golden Dawn —sharing a legacy of antiquity only with the original revival Orders and Lodges of Freemasons and Rosicrucians, all of which shared a common bond in England.

In the year 1717, modern Druidism was officially reintroduced to public consciousness and lodges of Freemasonry began to emerge—now permitting "Free" and "Accepted" *masons* into their ranks, those who were not actually "masons" by trade. Since the "Anti-Witchcraft" law-acts of England were still in place, members of such organizations were warned to openly show only an "intellectual" and "academic" interest in esoteric mysteries. They were cautioned regarding ramifications of socially misinterpreted intentions—as it was only a few years earlier, across "the pond," that puritans burned "witches" in Salem. Thus, many early "occult organizations" operated as charitable community groups, ecological activist foundations, natural history fellowships or national heritage societies.

Growing archaeological interest in ancient Celtic sites—along with scholarly "antiquarian" revival of related lore—inspired a renaissance of European "Celtic Reconstructionism," which led directly to modern neodruidism. Of course, the "universal bond" first professed by these neodruids was quickly abandoned after personal inclinations led to a series of schisms and separations—each forming a new "reformed" branch of the original tree—something that continues to present times, lending to the idea that modern Druidism is quite "political."

John Toland, a philosophical writer in England, founded the first modern Druid Order in 1717—based on his own personal researches—"The British Druid Circle of the Universal Bond" ["*An*

Druidh Uileach Braithreaches" (ADUB)]. Its tradition spread under the official banner name: "The Ancient Druid Order" (ADO). John Toland also published a discourse titled "Pantheisticon" in 1720—along with its related work "Clidophorus" —providing a handbook for "Hermetic Philosophical Societies" based on external (exoteric) and internal (esoteric) doctrines of the ancients.[*] He also included a script for group participation in what he defines as a *secret* "Socratic Society."

Use of the term "Pantheism" has grown over the past few centuries, now applied to an entire spectrum of arcane teachings and beliefs—as if to catch all that our society does not readily understand of them. Because the word so closely relates to the way we tend to categorize mythological systems of "gods"—as "pantheons"—there is a common misconception that the two terms are synonymous or literally describing one another. It is certainly not the same as what others have classified "polytheism."

John Toland coined the term "pantheism" in 1705, describing the philosophical paradigm of *Spinoza*

---

[*] A revised tercentenary edition of *Pantheisticon* was prepared by Joshua Free for the Mardukite Esoteric Library Archives and Systemology Society. It also appears in the appendix section of "*Merlyn's Complete Book of Druidism*" and "*The Complete Mardukite Master Course*."

—a doctrine that identifies "God" or *divinity* with the whole of the Universe—All-as-One. As revealed in the "Pantheisticon," this Secret Doctrine, observing the "Universal Law" animating and acting upon all things, is actually one-to-one with the "Esoteric Truth" known among learned "secret societies" and sects evolving from the "Ancient Mystery School." But, it is not the same as the outer public "Exoteric truths" vulgarly thrown about and debated on the "surface world" or "Realm" of the masses.

Pantheism is named for a "divine energy" imbuing and encompassing All Things and the "Cosmic Law" that dictates the natures of All Things—including their energetic interactions with each other. As expressed in modern or NexGen "Systemology"—no *Thing* exists in exclusion to all *Things*. This truth exists at all levels—those we observe causally and even those we only see effects from. It exists independent of human belief and whims of fantasy, yet is responsible for sparking both. It was observed among elite classes of the ancient world just as it has been carried forth into modern "New Age" systems via mystic traditions of revived Freemasonry, Rosicrucianism—and in the case of John Toland: Antiquarian Neodruidism. His works demonstrates that the pursuit of true knowledge must be protected by the secret societies and not perverted by the masses. He quotes *Seneca*, saying "When every man chooses to believe rather than judge, life is never brought to a scrutiny. Error is handed down father-to-son. And it is the dull infatuation of being led by the examples of others, that exposes us to ruin."

Some "Mesopagan Druids," like Henry Hurle—a member of Toland's early ADO—believed that the mysteries of the Druids extended beyond Celtic subjects. Hurle viewed neodruidism as an extension, if not a purely Celtic equivalent, to Eurasian Freemasonry, which was simultaneously revived in England in 1717—and indeed, at the same "Apple Tree Tavern" Toland revived Druidry. Coincidence?

Henry Hurle led a formation of the "Ancient Order of Druids" (AOD) in 1781. It extensively emphasized subjects relevant to his own background—Freemasonry, Rosicrucianism and the Kabbalah. These are the same fundamentals behind our more popularized versions of dispersal—the Aurum Solis or Golden Dawn type organizations with a lean toward Judaic mysticism. Some of the members, however, disliked this overt "occult" focus that the organization took on—preferring participation in more "neutrally" aligned groups. Many such "protestant" members formed their own AOD branch, returning to the vision maintained previously by John Toland, calling themselves the "United Ancient Order of Druids" (UAOD) in 1833. Other Masonic-based Druids banded together in 1874 under direction of Robert Wentworth Little, and formed the "Ancient Archaeological Order of Druids" (AAOD), later changing its name in 1886 to "Ancient Masonic Order of Druids" (AMOD).

In the 19th century, while quasi-Masonic Druidism developed, a separate nationalist-based movement grew alongside it. These reconstructionists sought to re-investigate Druidry as a "Bardic Tradition"—specifically preservation of disappearing national customs and languages in Wales (on the British Isle). Iolo Morganwg—compiler of the Welsh "Barddas" and "Pheryllt" manuscripts, among many others—pioneered the effort. Later, William Blake and Edward Davies also desired to preserve the language and "Druidism" of Wales for posterity. These traditions and customs, not to mention the common use of Welsh language was on the decline. This movement led to a revival of the "Gorsedd of Bards" gathering as part of the "National Eisteddfodd" festival still held annually to celebrate the arcane legacy of Wales.

Students of Druidism studying the subject of Welsh Bardism will be confronted by a myriad of controversial debate among the literature supplied by our contemporaries. Here we begin to see political issues arise regarding legitimacy of materials or claims of authenticity. Many of Iolo Morganwg's writings also appear under his given name

Edward Williams, or as attributed to Llywelyn Sion. Although many of these writings came under academic scrutiny later, they remain indispensable contributions to understanding Celtic mythology and Druidism. In fact, these controversial *Iolo Manuscripts*, including the *Myvyrian Archaeology* anthology and *Barddas*, are the main source for an abundant wealth of surviving Welsh materials—including the *Mabinogion*, *Hanes Taliesin*, *Cad Goddeu*, the *Gwarchans* and, of course, the Welsh or *"Cymric"* Triads, all of which are used throughout various neodruidic revivals. In one such manuscript, translated by Meyryg Davydd from the library of Raglan Castle, we find the true motive behind these collective revivalist efforts:--

> "It must be premised that the Bards are strictly enjoined by the rules of their Order to preserve and hand down intact all the memorials of their ancestors. The most abstruse questions connected with their system are committed exclusively to their care, professedly lest a too vulgar handling of them should cause them to be misunderstood and corrupted. Whether such a pretext would hold good in the present day may fairly be doubted; and it were well for the *Glamorgan Bards*, the sole deposits of these secrets, to consider whether they would not be better preserved, and withal prove more practically valuable, if commi-

64

tted to print, than left to the oral care of a
few individuals, who, however faithful
themselves, may not have successors of
equal trustworthiness. We are convinced
that there is nothing in the fundamental
principles of Bardism that requires a per-
petual reserve. There are several things
now published, which were once looked
upon as bardic secrets..."

Organized neodruidism did not reach America until the early 1900's as an extension of AAOD/
AMOD. While once a quasi-Masonic secret society, the "Ancient Order of Druids in America"
(AODA) has evolved into a standard "green magic" system under the current direction of author,
John Michael Greer, including emphasis on elements from his own background, such as sacred
geometry and the Golden Dawn. In the 1960's, students at Carleton College (Minnesota) launched
the neodruidic religion as a rebellious act to
counter a college requirement of church participation—thus, the "Reformed Druids of North America" (RDNA) was born, and is still in existence
today.

Ross Nichols enjoyed membership in ADO for a
decade when Arch Druid Robert MacGregor Reid
passed away in 1963. This caused a schism among
remaining members concerning the election of a
new "Chosen Chief"—a preferred title in some

branches of Druidry as opposed to "Arch Druid." Many of the ADO members at that time agreed with Nichols that emphasis on "Theosophical" and "Rosicrucian" approaches to Druidry did not seem very "Druidic"—so in 1964, he formed the "Order of Bards, Ovates & Druids" (OBOD). The Order did originally maintain some "Eastern" flavors—based on the inclined background of its founder—but the group remained mainly *Celtic* with an emphasis on the Bardic Arts. As a result, the group lists "Bard" as its "First Degree," contrary to the "Ovate" or "Novitiate" degree being the first historically.

After his death, control of OBOD was passed down from Nichols to its most recent Chosen Chief, Philip Carr-Gomm. Back in America, 1980's fantasy sub-culture accompanied growing interest in neopagan revival, causing the Reformed Druidism of North America to evolve into increasingly more serious revival movements toward the modern practice of Druidry.

One branch of RDNA famously evolved through the efforts of the late Isaac Bonewits—founder of "A Druid Fellowship" (ADF) in America, incorporating influences from his own background in traditional witchcraft. In spite of its questionable founder, ADF sparked the beginnings of a larger Druidic network in the United States, the first to be comparable in any way with OBOD in England

and Council of British Druid Orders (COBDO). ADF and OBOD became international successes —both Philip Carr-Gomm and Issac Bonewits reached critical heights as exponent public authorities on "contemporary" Druidism. In the interim, however, several ADF members broke away in 1986 to form perhaps the largest offshoot of the American Druid trunk—the Henge of Keltria (HK), originally based in Minnesota (the home of RDNA) for a time. Henge of Keltria primarily sought to remove the excessive "Wiccan" influence that overran ADF materials.

In the 1980's, Douglas Monroe, an esoteric Druidologist, began to lay the foundations for his "New Forest Centre of Magickal Studies," with a Druid curriculum emphasizing the Arthurian and Welsh themes, using the "Pheryllt" paradigm as a reference point. This work is laid out across a trilogy of materials—*The 21 Lessons of Merlyn*, *Lost Books of Merlyn* and *Deepteachings of Merlyn*. What we now call "Mardukite Druidology" is a holistic extension of Monroe's work coupled with esoteric archeology of Mesopotamian and other European regions that contribute to our total awareness of this ancient "systemology."

So many instances appear in neodruidic legacy where attitudes, tones, themes, philosophical and spiritual emphasis of one Druid group or another are all based on inclinations and background of its founding members. Consequently, a modern pursuit of Druidry has become fractured into a myriad of interpretive forms—a prismatic display of variegated lights—abandoning *Seekers* to discretely discern the true core of the wisdom, like a search for the diamond in the rough. It is the current hope that this *Druid's Handbook* will shine a clearer light for one to conduct their searches on the Druid Path.

DOCTRINES OF DRUIDISM

Nearly synonymous with what is now popularly considered "Celtic" in the New Age, the ancient "Bardic Tradition" served as an integral part of Druidic systemology—its instruction and preservation throughout history. With the destruction of the Druids themselves, those freely wandering Bardic Wizards and masters of disguise were able to survive the cultural genocide of Keltia and maintain roots to a distant stream of wisdom.

Traditionally, the Bardic class wore azure blue cloaks for ceremonial observations and earth-toned colors during everyday work. Publicly in the Druid Order, Bards often served as "Heralds of the Procession" during festival celebrations. They are not only the authors and writers of poetry and music, but the performers of the same, meant to set the mood and charge the general atmosphere of the rituals with their creative energies. "Bardic verses" have passed down to us through mythological sources, revealing glimpses to the wisdom of their teachings.

Bards studied natural sciences and philosophies, often relating them to what is best classified as "elemental magic," but these principles demonstrated an understanding of universal energy and Cosmic Law. Traditional artists and historians frequently depict Bardic Druids as archetypal "wizards," all clad in blue—the color of the skies—and even donning a conical Anunnaki-inspired "phyrgian cap" decorated with astrological glyphs in the same manner as the Persian Magi. Beyond this, Bards were responsible for studying and memorizing the core doctrines and triad teachings of Druidic systemology, as part of a rigorous training period that, according to some records, could extend to as much as 20 years in the "Bardic College."

The "Chief Doctrines" of Druidic Tradition are not viewed by modern neodruids as a "code of laws" in the traditional sense. In some ways they appear outdated and no longer practical for execution in the modern world—we are no longer obviously residing in ancient *Keltia*. Therefore, as a model for our modern pursuit of Druidry, they are important historical fundamentals—a primer of the metaphysics and metapsychology existent within the ancient Druidic methodology.

1. DOCTRINE OF SEPARATIONS

Energetically, a destructive interference is likely to occur in mixed genders—specifically concerning energy flow between individuals. The sexes are programmed to operate attuned to different vibrations. This makes it difficult for a complete circuit (*circulation*) of energy to take place.

Children trained with Druids (or in Druidism) are schooled in like-gender environments with curriculum designed specific to the learning style of that gender. Druids educated males and females separately—each sent to a Druidic school in a remote location, independent of one another and free from gender-based distraction. Remains of some male schools were found on Anglessey, Iona and Ynys Wyth (Isle of Wight), and the most famous of female colleges was in Avalon—now Glastonbury.

"New Age" metaphysical teachings do acknowledge that each gender operates on different polarities of energy in our dualistic universal experience —a constant cycle of sending out (projecting) and receiving energy based on the structure or programmed nature of the respective polarity. In this way, "polarity" can be seen as a metaphysical "filter" to the experience of our constant projection and receipt of energy. This energetic transference, exchange or communication of forces is what constitutes "reality" on the part of the "Observer." It is how we perceive or internalize our objective experience, or rather how we interact and relate to encounters with external energies and forces. Consider this following "energy flow equation"—an illustrative method the current author uses to demonstrate the "systemology" of various teachings:

$$(x) \rightarrow [+/-] \rightarrow \{EGO\} \rightarrow [+/-] \rightarrow (y)$$
(x) = energy received
(y) = energy projected
{EGO} = "I" of the Observer

From a relatively "wider encompassing perspect-ive" these polarities—as well as polar dualism in general—do not actually exist and are only per-ceptual illusions or glamours fueling relative movement of the 3D physical expression of the universe. We must have ebbs and flows—the movement of tides—for the "things" to exist, but beneath the surface, it is all the same encom-passing ocean. We tend to associate with its most concrete peaks into our awareness, leaving valleys between waves that are beneath or outside our normative sensual parameters.

More than simple "gender separation" in the phys-ical sense, deeper wisdom of this truth is found hidden within this "doctrine." and even revealing elements of a subsequent "Doctrine of Like-Aspects," where incorporation of "like-energies" in Druid magic are a means of maintaining or pre-serving more highly concentrated flows of specific unadulterated energy. By keeping polarity isolated, a stronger bond with a specific energy current could be achieved.

Ancient Babylonian-influenced and Pythagoreanstyled Druids with keen interests in mathematics came to discover another unique quality concerning the unity of polar opposites. If one sought to unite them as a balanced force, they would, in turn, cancel each other out. We can demonstrate this quantification in wave patterns or even more simply with integers on a line. This observation led to the "Doctrine of Imbalances," which explains how perfectly balanced oppositional forces will allow for the net sum of zero. If we consider an axis or polar line segment such as:

---|---|---|---|---|---|---|---
-3 -2 -1 0 +1 +2 +3

Now consider the following mathematical example, correctly stated as:

$$(-3) + (+3) = 0$$

2. DOCTRINE OF AUTHORITY

The true quest of mastery is one of the Self—and in that Self-Honest discipline, cumulative mastery of what is perceived as apart from or external to Self; and then only by living a realization that the Self and ALL are One. True authority is achieved only with discipline, meaning "self-discipline." This is a Self-directed authority—the I AM operating and controlling all of its faculties consciously. Emotional self-control and authority requires emotional discipline. Psychological or mental authority and prowess requires mental discipline.

Logic endorsing this sentiment conjures a deeply laden "Doctrine of Like-Aspects" once again. It suggests that like-forces will—at their "highest" level—attract other like-forces. Positive movement and true growth exists through a combination of like-terms, which we can illustrate (again) using mathematical models. Allowing (+) to be any "positive integer"—or number value—and (−) to be any "negative integer," the resulting sum (or product) of this combinatorial exchange will always be "positive."

$$(+) + (+) = + \qquad (-) + (-) = +$$
$$(+) \times (+) = + \qquad (-) \times (-) = +$$

These cases always apply. Other operations are unimportant for this application because they do not seek to increase the total value of the whole. Scientists and mathematicians are able to recognize the same principles in wave frequency interaction —lending to either a positive or negative interference pattern. Changing these equations with a union of polar opposites will result in a negative sum (product) or decline/ decrease every time. Application of this principle is not exclusive to only mathematical interpretations.

Every idea and principle related to lessons from

the Ancient Mystery School—and even the modern "New Thought" movement—suggests that our "thoughts are things" just as much as anything we might assign the title "physical" to other things. Thoughts produce like-manifestations. Energy from the "internal" faculties of the mind is projected and experienced in the "outer" environment, and this is only natural—a part of Cosmic Law—since at the "highest level" or clearest point of all encompassing awareness, the two are not separate. Individual expectations, emotional charges and even physical behaviors all contribute to the universal energetic flow— which people often call the "vibrations."

Experiential knowledge is a result or product of interactions with some existing relative factor—or it would have no meaning. You could not build a "house" without first internalizing a concept or archetype of "house" in your mind's eye. Without a frame of reference for such a semantic or concept, the whole idea of "house" would be non-existent to you—meaning not within your *"realm,"* or *"reality."*

The more examples of "house" you witness, the greater your "experience" becomes with the concept and the greater number of possible "pictures" held in the mind. This does not dismiss the idea of creating new things—though many innovations are really enhancements or alterations of an existing archetype. Everything that can be manifested in the world of forms already exists in the world of thought, and they are one. Consider how these principles would apply to our current Druidic methods of instruction directly. The (a) value will, for our purposes, be a singular Bardic lesson.

(a1) → {EGO} → (a2)
(a1) = lesson given from teacher to student
(a2) = lesson reinterpreted from student
{EGO} = student the formula is calculated for

The instructor observes the student's learning process until the introduced variable (a) has been completely internalized and reproduced—given the personalization of the student—to a satisfactory standard. The variable (a) must be completed (as a cycle) before new variables of supplemental learning will be introduced.

Cumulative education programs are designed to supplement preexisting knowledge rather than replace it or consistently change its focus. In unstructured modes of academia, new learning often interferes with the recall and use of old learning. In the next doctrine, the total sum of the parts [$a + b + c$] is impossible to figure until we have a value for each variable separately—but this is how "Mystery Schools" are gauged.

3. DOCTRINE OF INSTRUCTION

The curriculum, to be effective, must always be personalized to an individual student. Close monitoring of an initiate's process is critical. The subsequent grades (for example, b), shall not be administered until aptitude is proven in a current level of learning (*a*). There is also a strict enforcement in "Mystery Schools" concerning the communication of subsequent knowledge (*b*) among students (or other initiates) who are not yet officially being administered that (*b*) grade.

In some Druid schools this philosophy is a part of the "Doctrine of Critical Periods," wherein children are acknowledged as possessing unique learning abilities generally disappearing with age. Thus, Druids would closely watch children of the Celts, taking interest in any demonstrating special aptitude—s those who seemed to "shine" above the rest. "Gifted youth" were usually spirited away into seclusion at Druid Colleges or given private instruction in remote locations—outside regular reach of townspeople of urbanized society. Therefore private educations also took place in small huts and forest groves. In such places, "high minds" among the Celts were reared separately and installed into positions of power and authority within Celtic civilization. For this reason, some classical renderings attributed to Druids the title of "Father of the Celts."

In accordance with the laws of apprenticeship, a master or private tutor could only have one (*a*) student and one (*b*) student simultaneously. The (*c*) curriculum—that which was possessed by the master—was typically only administered by more centrally governed Druidic Colleges, sanctuaries located on islands or within dense woods. The concept of [*a + b + c*] can easily be used for our purposes to reflect the three traditional "degrees" of Druidism—the Ovate, Bard and Derwydd (Druid) respectively. However, since the lessons of each are actually cumulative, it would be more accurate to illustrate the academic development in the following formula:

$$[\, a \,] \rightarrow [\, a(b) \,] \rightarrow [\, ab(c) \,] = [\, abc \,]$$

4. DOCTRINE OF MNEMONICS

We cannot argue that the lore and wisdom attained through pursuits of Druidry are better experienced, internalized and committed to memory, rather than open it to profane scrutiny by the uninitiated through writing. True Knowledge is to be accessed by direct experience and put into practice by intuition—maybe only then intellectualized and analyzed in text.

Without direct experience, many limitations exist in sole relay of available languages and semantic terminology. There are some aspects of the cosmos

—lessons learned by Druids from Nature—that are nearly incommunicable with ordinary words. It is clear that ancient Druids recognized this limitation in language and its social definitions; for example, the semantics or "meanings" literally attached to or associated with any usage of "vocabulary" and "terminology." If we were to restrict our learning and understanding to only a primitive use of written or verbal expressions—such as the words on this page—we would, every time, fall short of grasping the true experience, true knowledge and true wisdom available to us in Nature.

5. DOCTRINE OF IMBALANCES

"From the point of greatest imbalance comes the point of greatest stability." The continuous development in what is considered the weakest point will provide for a steady and well-balanced growth pattern. This philosophy is established to assist the initiate in succeeding in each aspect of the "liberal arts" presented through each of the grades of personal development. Keep in mind: the ultimate and most lofty purpose or motivation behind a pursuit of Druidry is for *Self-actualization*. In practical applications, when there are two areas of focus and one is notably accelerated and one is weaker, a focus on the weaker will help to balance the forces —or distribution of knowledge and skill—when the two are combined.

Imagine building a brick wall. If you assembled one side of the wall much quicker than the other side, then building up the lower side later becomes more difficult, almost impossible to manage or much weaker. Imagine jumping from one pillar to another beside it as both are continually moving apart from one another. The challenge level increases drastically as the apparent difference and distance between the two platforms increases or elevates with one pillar higher than the other.

6. DOCTRINE OF MYSTERY SCHOOLS

By heavily guarding the secrets of the universe from the naïve population, the Universal Truth and Cosmic Law dispersed exclusively by the Mystery School could be maintained. Druid "fellowships" and "schools" formed, composed by members working together in their own "societies" to protect the integrity of these mysteries. It is a necessity in our world that we should have to explore the path toward Truth and Ascension in isolation or only amongst a small segment of the masses. By sharing and discovering within the confines of the "Mystery School"—or, as is described elsewhere, a "Socratic society"— one can work toward these pursuits safely and without fear of reproach by the larger segment of uninitiated society that does not carry the same awareness—and experience pool—to properly understand and relate to the mysteries. "All things ought not to be declared to all men," explains John Toland. He continues, in his introduction to the "Pantheisticon":

> "We shall be in safety," says Seneca, "if we separate ourselves from the Multitude; for the Multitude," as the same author indicates a little after, "is a proof of what is worst"—and "nothing is so vulgar," in the opinion of Tully, "as to have no relish for knowledge." Therefore, "Philosophy," to continue use of Tully's words, "contents itself with a few Judges; it designedly shuns the Multitude, as conscious of its jealousy and hatred."

> "For your part, learned and ingenious reader, if you choose to follow Reason, rather than Custom, for your guide, you shall repute all human casualties to be placed in a degree far beneath you; you shall, patiently take up with your lot, whatever it is; you shall keep foolish ambition and gnawing envy at a distance from you; you shall despise perishable honors, being to perish yourself in a short time; you shall lead a peaceable and pleasant Life, neither admiring nor dreading any Thing."

Since the beginning of human civilization—notably originating in the Ancient Near East (or Mesopotamia)—we see visibly in history, a unique and almost "elite" minority percentage of society, individuals that are considered the "Enlightened" or "Illuminated" or "those who know." A long-standing tradition of various "underground cabals" and "secret societies" have existed in nearly all times and places to protect these people, although there are certainly many who have gone forth in public —out of phase with the times—and been subject to all varieties of nasty fate. Even in secluded, aboriginal and tribal communities, the secrets of "shamanism" are those that only the "shaman"— and someone apprenticed to them—knows.

7. DOCTRINE OF THE ENLIGHTENED

When a child is visibly prodigious beyond their years, the knowledge and intuition can give way to wisdom at an early age. When a child pursues wisdom via the "Quest for Absolute Truth," then the "real wisdom" will be more likely to remain into adulthood. These tendencies should be encouraged as soon as they are discovered, because when the focus of youth turns toward more "worldly matters," then such a focus will usually remain fixed into adulthood.

This doctrine might also go forth to explain the concept of the "mid-life crisis" sometimes experienced by adults. Consider a person that is realizing that half or more of their life—and their prime and able years—is now behind them. They begin to reflect on their physical and spiritual legacy—about what true "advancements" they have achieved during this lifetime: the differences made; the mark on the world; the attainment of personal pursuits; the acquisition of the true key to Ascension when passing through the gates of this world, &tc. True spirituality, in this way, is not concerned with "religion" in the traditional sense, but instead represents one's own personal relationship with the "Source of All Being and Creation," in whatever manner the individual understands this "force."

The "Doctrine of the Enlightened Child" corresponds directly with the "Doctrine of Critical Periods" and what is called the "clean-slate theory" in contemporary psychology. Before a young Druid is exposed to the kaleidoscope of forms available as "worldly" stimuli, they are trained, instructed in the Druid crafts and systematically strengthened for their personal individual path. They are privileged to receive unhindered means to reach their highest potential—and then only after this are they permitted to go and express this individuality out in the world-at-large, adding personal strength to that of the community. Without this aid, the path of self-discovery is still attainable, but often marked with greater social challenges when energetically interacting in a world where many masks and facades must be artificially created and worn in order to survive and play out a myriad of "roles."

We know now that there are indeed critical periods of learning attached to the human condition. A child is much more capable, for example, of learning multiple languages with ease than an adult who has become more fixed in their wiring. One gets accustomed to seeing the world through a specific lens of "truth," and the longer we do so, the harder it is to adjust our vision to the real "Truth."

Let us consider the example of "magic." In Druidry, "magic" is essentially a "mind-set"—a mental baseline systemology that maintains a greater awareness of energy and Cosmic Law. This is not particularly well understood by the general population—or "Multitudes" dominating the "surface world" or "Realm." Therefore, such knowledge is classified "mysterious," "esoteric" or "occult"— and this relates to everything once originally in the domain of the "Ancient Mystery School." Many of these once "secrets" are now taken for granted as "basic facts" in our world today, but they were once considered "magical" and studied exclusively beneath the surface of the "norm."

Much of what separates a "magical" classification of "reality," versus what is perceived by the "norm," might be reduced to a combination of what we have previously described: a vigilant and/ or awakened holistic awareness mixed with an appropriate use of fixed semantics, vocabulary and language to process information internally and articulate it—or express it—where appropriate. The strange irony here remains that all of the matters and "Things" explored by conventional sciences and philosophies are the same "Things" or phenomenon treated in the "occult realm" of "esoteric knowledge." Differences lie only in the ability to apply the different "levels of understanding" to an all-encompassing semantic or understanding. We cannot examine "parts" in exclusion to all other "parts." Our understanding of Universal Truth must apply equally—united and interconnected to all aspects of Cosmic Law. Nothing can be treated in "exclusion."

Our current doctrine exists to remind us that critical thinking and abilities to be artistically creative are both products of an enlightened child. Sometimes the two traits go hand in hand, but one tends to be expressed stronger than the other; hence the application of our "Doctrine of Imbalances" to assist facilitating growth in the direction that is more lacking. It appears that these traits, when nurtured, significantly aid the individual progression along the Path through adulthood and especially in the face of more difficult social challenges and situations of life where these states of accomplishment are more difficult to attain (and/or maintain) if at all.

The question still remains as to whether "enlightenment" is a state or ability that all humans innately possess—raising questions about the human condition, and the degree of influence we have in our "nature" and the contributory effects of our "environment." Examination of Druidic lore would suggest that they held the opinion that human beings traveled a path between these two factors: who they are genetically and who they are spiritually. Consider the potential of a child "enlightened" from birth, but strengthened and nurtured by the proper "environment." Or the opposite: an unrecognized and uncultured prodigious child thwarted in their advancement.

8. DOCTRINE OF THE SPHERES

The Universe, both the visible and unseen parts of the continuous spectrum—sometimes called "dimensions"—operates according to the "Doctrine of the Spheres," known elsewhere in lore as the "Druid's Cabala."

The three primary "spheres" cohabit the same points in space as we understand it, though they exist at "levels" perceived as "above" and "below" the normative range of the spectrum. We only directly acknowledge experience from a portion of reality while interacting with physical geography and forms that the human 3-D condition is "wired" or "programmed" to receive awareness from. Philosophically the spheres are all One, but semantically each of the spheres exists at a different "vibration" or "frequency."

Although our experience with the existence of all dimensions or levels might lead us to perceived them as independently separate from one another, they are actually all connected in wholeness—All-as-one. Energies from one "level" can and will affect another "level." At the highest point of connectivity, they are the same plane. Energy seems to travel between by "unobserved" means, or using some medium we experience as other that what it actually is, but manifesting on this plane as something in our awareness. This is called "*perturbation.*"

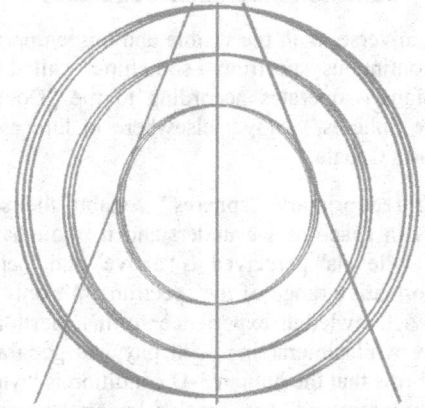

Rooted in ancient philosophy and Bardic verses, the "Three Spheres" model recognized by modern

Druids was popularized during the "Antiquarian Druidism" movement. It appears in the Welsh manuscript entitled "*Barddas,*" and although the text and its author are a point of controversy, the doctrines seem to have infiltrated modern Druidism nonetheless. Even the "tribann" or "Three Rays" glyph now iconic to Druidry first emerge from the Welsh Bardic revival of Iolo Morganwg. As a cosmological model of existence, this lore is sometimes referred to as the "Druid's Cabala," because it shares some similarity with the Babylonian and Semitic Kabbalah. Traditionally the spheres or "Circles of Existence" are depicted as a three concentric rings. They are defined—from the inside, out—as *Abred*, *Gwynedd* and *Ceugent*.

THE FIRST SPHERE—ABRED

ABRED is the smallest "circle" ("sphere") of existence plotted on the Druid's Cabala, enveloping the "Cauldrons of Annwn" (pronounced "ah-noon"), the "pool" or realm of elementary minerals, atoms and particulates—the basic requirements for physical existence and the infinite potential of its expression. The "Middle Earth"—as humans understand it—is the circle of Abred, the "Realm of Matter," home of the animal, plant/tree and human kingdoms.

The sphere of Abred is the smallest because the part of the continuous spectrum that is experienced at this "level" is refined, fragmented and restricted to the most condensed states of energetic experience. According to the Druidic Tradition, an entity can spend several incarnations (or "rebirths") in Abred—even existing in forms that are other than human in order to learn, experience and naturally evolve along the Universal Path of Ascension. All of our different lessons, experiences and choices, contribute toward or against our current ability to ascend from the gravity of this heavy world toward a permanent transition into *Gwynedd*.

All existence and all beings making residence on Abred first emerges from the "Cauldron of Annwn"—is fragmented as an "identity" from the infinite pool, and must progressively master survival through the rigid material existence. Cosmic Law is fixed and all energy and existence must abide by it. Then we are subjected to "laws" of the other Realms... the "law of the jungle" in the animal kingdom... the "laws of game theory and systemology" in the human kingdom... all the while reaching toward our highest evolution and a return to the Source.

When lessons and challenges are not mastered—when the individual succumbs too greatly to glamours of artificial forms and laws of their kingdom —a person may find themselves entangled in one of life's man "vicious cycles." Once examining the nature of these, we discover they are rooted in "mental programming" coded by "emotional imprints," and there is no apparent lack of "Self-Help" avenues and "No-Help" groups and gurus promoted in today's market as a means to resolve this. Many of these are rooted on valid "New Thought" precepts, but were later corrupted into complex organizational hierarchies and profit-driven enterprises.*

Barddas material does not glorify existence in the "physical world"—"*cylch yr Abred*"—because dependencies and pitfalls that distract spiritual progress (for those actually seeking it) are more numerous in Abred than anywhere else in creation. But if the "freedom" to pursue one's own destiny ("program") and the resources (environment) are permitting, a spiritually-governed entity (human or otherwise) has a naturally tendency—or inclination—to return to its Source; to the point of highest realization, understanding, awareness and existence.

Teachings of the Bardic Tradition describe the pools of Annwn as a dark swirling Abyss; a cauldron; a melting pot of primordial elements swirling about. . . It is not, however, portrayed as an "Underworld" or "Land of the Dead"—such as we might find in other cosmological models. Rather,

---

* "Mardukite Systemology" is recommended as an effective alternative. See, for example, "*Crystal Clear*" and "*Imaginomicon*" by Joshua Free.

the "primordial abyss" or "Cauldron" is a place of *origins*—a world of birth and renewal—recycling the energy that has come from the Source. It is not a destination after death, except that fragmented beings so formed will magnetically return to "re-form" until they have broken the energetic gravitational pull of Abred as "Ascension."

Following with other Cosmic Laws in effect, Abred keeps what is its own within its Realm by the tendency of physical energetic conservation—but the physical component is only one aspect of our "Identity." What we consider the most "solid" portions of our "Self"—and which are not the Self, but only a vehicle for it to interact in this environment—will always "fall back down" to its own common level, but when the strong bonds held to this state are broken, the Self may effectively escape the "pull down" to a inevitable mutual starting point with the "body" and achieve the next or "higher" level of manifestation as the "common baseline." The journey does not end there; but we have successfully "graduated" Abred.

The purpose of any spiritual being is to successfully survive their navigation of the interdimensional labyrinth of creation, and the lessons found in each aspect of that existential experience, while following a pathway that returns to the Source. The Realm of Abred is essentially where you are materializing your conscious existence at this very moment. Many spiritual beings and "Ascended Masters" have visited, learned from and contributed to this "Earth School" throughout the ages. But most creatures have given in to the "once-born animus" mentality, becoming slaves to the senses and sharing in only a limited range of potential physical existence.

THE SECOND SPHERE—GWYNEDD

GWYNEDD (pronounced "gweneth") is the "middle sphere" or "second circle" of existence—not to be confused with lore of "Middle-Earth" or "mid-Branch," which is actually Abred. Unlike more contemporary worldviews held regarding life and death in orthodox traditions today, the "Druid's Cabala" does not depict Gwynedd as a permanent resting place after death in this life—although it is the Realm that "encompasses" the circle of Abred, and ultimately the "direction" we are Ascending to. But rather, Gwynedd is a transitional place during the progressive journey of a spiritual being that has escaped the hold of an otherwise restricted manifestation of the "material realm."

Where Bardic lore suggests that the "*cylch y Gwynedd*" is best equated with what we call the "spirit realm," "Otherworld," "astral plane" and even "elemental" and "faerie" kingdoms. This semantics has suggested to some individuals that the Gwynedd "level" of existence is "supernatural" or less "physical" or "material" or even "real" than the Realm of Forms we identify as Abred. This is not the case. By whatever title it is known by, "Gwynedd" exists everywhere around us but at a degree of relative vibration that is simply beyond the identification of third-dimensional creation in Abred. The same basic energies and elements of *Life* and *Awareness* exist simultaneously in both realms and they are interconnected. As spiritual "Identities" occupying a human vehicle for material existence, we are often limited to experiencing universal forces via the sensory perception of a "body" tuned to share in a communication with the frequencies on the Abred "band" of wavelengths.

Our journey through Abred eventually carries us to Gwynedd, but it is not the "highest" or most unified plane united with the Source. In Gwynedd, the spirit-soul is still a singular fragmented "Identity" with the ability to continue learning new lessons that compliment those uncovered in previous experiences of Abred. These lessons are now able to be explored and mastered in a new environment, relatively less restrictive in its fluid energy than in Abred. Certain memories—or more correctly, "imprints" on consciousness—are still carried (transitioned) to other successive "levels" of existence. Only those beings attaining perfection in Gwynedd can rise "above" (ascend) to the "Sphere" of Ceugent—"Infinity."

A combination of mental and spiritual faculties coupled with the metaphysical equivalent of "genetic memory" attached to the Identity, are the seeker's primary tools when working in Gwynedd. This psychologically oriented domain also holds the "Hall of Records," an etheric imprint of all potential courses of energetic interaction that materials from the "New Age" community often refer to as the "Akashic Library." It is the belief of many practitioners that this Realm is mentally accessible while still residing in Abred.

Bardic Tradition describes Gwynedd as "free of evil, desire and death," which makes it an ideal environment to devote existence to personal spiritual development. As the second of three main "divisions" present within the Druid's Cabala, Gwynedd is another "school"—greatly improved from what we experience in Abred. Life is not perfect in Gwynedd—but it is refined energy that contributes to personal spiritual energetic refinement. Just as Abred resonates within a certain range allowing one to access Gwynedd, so too can we find a wave to ride the highest frequencies of Gwynedd to Ceugent. This is the opportunity provided in the "Otherworld"—a direct bridge back to the Source for those with enough knowledge to seek it; and enough Will to see themselves across it.

Just as thoughts, actions and energy exchanges in

our present world of Abred will either lend toward
or against our journey to Gwynedd, the "goals" or
"virtues" of Gwynedd—listed in the "*Barddas*"—
are perfect love, perfect peace and perfect knowledge. That which is perfect, ineffable and absolute, by logic and definition, will lead us to the
Highest—to the ALL.

THE THIRD SPHERE—CEUGENT

Ceugent is the "infinite" realm, that which extends
within and throughout all spatial dimensions and
times simultaneously. It envelops all relative pres-
ences in the lower realms, entangling and intercon-
necting all existences at the "highest energetic
level" of creation. Bardic Lore from the Druid's
Cabala describes "*cylch y Ceugent*" as the very domain of the Source of All-Being and Creation—
the place where all beings ascend and reunite with
the Source. Much of this energy is recursively
funneled back via the infinite spiral to the "Cauldron of Annwn" and recycled into new forms of existence; manifestations of fundamental expression
in the circle of Abred.

We consider each plane of existence in this model
"vibrating" its existence at a particular "frequency" (a range or parameter within the continuous
spectrum). Therefore, a spiritual being must achieve "spiritual perfection" or else the attainment of a
suitable "etheric vehicle" in Gwynedd by which to

move and travel and continue an ascent to the Source. Ceugent is a zone that only resonates true and Absolute "spiritual perfection"—a *unified field*" or state of awareness where ALL is experienced in perfect or total connection to ALL "other" existences—All-as One.

The Sphere of Ceugent is the largest outer ring represented by the Druid's Cabala—demonstrating that its very nature is all-encompassing force that will generally escape our Abred-limited perception of space-time, yet we instinctively know it is present all around us, and humanity uses every means available to search for it. The scientific implications are incredible, because this model suggests "big energy in small places." The energetic potential of matter is astronomical. The energetic potential of Ceugent is infinity.

DRUIDIC WISDOM TRIADS

I. THE 3 QUESTS OF MASTERY

a.) mastery of the self
b.) mastery of the physical
c.) mastery of the unknown

The first is a chronological triad in which successive stages of development are plotted out in an: *a, then b, then c,* schema. Though not all triads can be broken down into this energetic formula of accumulation, this one works nicely for this.

$$[\,abc\,] = [\,a\,] \rightarrow [\,a(b)\,] \rightarrow [\,ab(c)\,]$$

Consider that "mastery of the unknown" requires "mastery of the physical"; and "mastery of the physical" is dependent on a "mastery of the self." In this triad we can easily see a direct relationship between the parts. Each of the parts of the triad can be further broken down for comprehension.

a.) Authority in self-discipline, possession of true self-knowledge (self-honesty), the proper use of willpower, and exercising the influential power of the mind.

b.) Authority over one's personal environment, enlightenment through "true-knowledge," the power of the psyche as an extension of the Universe or "cosmic consciousness."

c.) Authority over the forces of the Universe, creating and maintaining an energetic communicative link with the 'Other' (or the Source), and finally the realization and manifestation of the 'godhead' within.

II. THE 3 VIRTUES OF WISDOM

a.) to be aware of all things
b.) to experience all things
c.) to be removed from all things

III. THE 3 KEYS TO TRANSCENDENCE

a.) see all
b.) study all
c.) experience all

Although expressing the same ideal, the previous triads come down from different schools of Druidry and two keywords expressed ("Wisdom" versus "Transcendence") carry different meaning. The triads explain the need to be an "Observer," to be witness to All but to remain separate and glean the "true-knowledge" from all experience in an objective way. From the combination of parts, we can deduce the following:

$$\text{WISDOM} = \{true\text{-}knowledge\} \times \{experience\} + \{objectivity\}$$

The triad expresses the need for detachment from

what is observed, for without this there really is no objective and logical viewpoint taken. Just as we see in contemporary "sciences," the Druid method of interpreting natural phenomenon also included what we call today "empirical observation" and the "scientific method."

IV. THE 3 KEYS TO DRUIDIC MASTERY

a.) to know
b.) to dare
c.) to remain silent

To know is to learn and take initiative toward comprehension. To dare is to use the knowledge that is learned and the utilization of 'true-knowledge' can result in wisdom. Wisdom will aid one in identifying the "Right Way" while on the Path.

This triad warns the initiate to remain silent about the work and study being conducted—also in regard to the Druidic Tradition presented as a "Mystery School." It is also important to note, concerning all New Age subjects—including ritual magic and "spellcraft"—that informing and discussing with non-related "uninitiated" persons deters the energetic purity of the link maintained between the magical operator and the goal.

Going about your (Druidic) work quietly will carry many personal benefits. When you can keep the "magical" things that happen to you to yourself, you help ensure they remain "magical" to you —personal and powerful. The enthusiasm and energy related to any experience can be emotionally "taken away" by others if you allow it—but it is up to you to allow it. Naturally, the disbelief from others can be a hard challenge.

V. THE 3 REQUIREMENTS FOR DRUID APPRENTICESHIP

a.) eyes that can truly see Nature
b.) a heart that can truly feel Nature
c.) clarity that can truly understand Nature

Druidry is a "Nature-oriented" Path to Ascension —often considered a "natural philosophy" far more than a blatant "occult tradition" in the common regard for these words. A true appreciation and empathy for the world of Nature is required for the Druid's Path—as evident in surviving art, prose and traditions from the ancient Druids and Celts. The "green world" of Nature played a significant role in their understanding of life and their interaction with creation. Druids concluded that inspiration from Nature was of the highest order and of utmost importance to all humanity—especially the Druidic initiate.

The clarity or resolution of the "matrix screen"— the way in which one views the world—must be "open" and "attuned" to follow the essence of what Nature (the Universe) actually is—in its state that we observe everyday, but also in its timeless and formless essence. It is this timeless quality that we chart as a "multiverse" of infinite possibilities.

VI. THE 3 OBJECTIVES OF BARDCRAFT

a.) to reform society
b.) to ensure peace in the land
c.) to preserve the excellence of the earth

Druids pride themselves on their abilities to manifest energetic change in the "external environment"—seeking to maintain peace and harmony (or balance) between people and the land throughout ancient Keltia with selective intervention. The Druids understood that knowledge lends to power, but that the application of power is tied to "responsibility"—or the ability to respond and communicate our intentions, to "be the change we want to see in the world."

Historically, the ancient Bards and Druids were able to come between rivaling tribes and prevent war. Then, after the battle ceased, Bards would come with their musical instruments and the voice to create an "air" of tranquility, while the Druids administered logical counsel to the leaders and soldiers. Druids seek, revere and maintain all that is beautiful, good and true on earth—and as such, maintain a respect for all Life.

VII. THE 3 LAWS OF APPRENTICESHIP

a.) a master may take only one per degree at a time

b.) a master must instruct the degrees separately

c.) the apprentices may not take apprentices

By limiting the "classroom" size of personal apprenticeship, Druids ensured that initiates would not slip through the academic process--rather, they would experience a significant amount of personal attention from a true mentor. The Druid Code—as illustrated from the surviving Welsh triad verses—restricted the number of possible apprentices a master could keep at once to two: one *Ovydd* noviciate and one *Bardd*. Some traditions observe the *Bardd* as the preliminary grade. When ready, first-degree students are permitted to enter the second degree of instruction and mentors sponsored second-degree apprentices for admittance to a more formal "Druid College."

During the Ovydd grade, initiates spend a great deal of time in seclusion—carrying their lessons and meditations into deep forests and wilderness to exercise them. This also frees up the attentions of the instructor—the *Derwydd* master—to dispense the elementary lessons—called "*gwers*" or "*gwersu*" plural—to a Bardic student. This triad law prevents Bardd and Ovydd initiates from taking on apprentices of their own—although they might be called upon to assist instructing or tutoring a peer. For example, a *Bardd* might be permitted to receive assistance from a fellow Bardd or another "higher degree" initiate.

VIII. THE 3 FOUNDATIONS OF THE HIGH COUNCIL

a.) truth in our hearts
b.) strength in our hands
c.) consistency in our tongues

IX. THE 3 CONDITIONS FOR LOSING A CHAIR ON THE COUNCIL

a.) performing murder or warfare
b.) telling a falsehood in council
c.) divulging the secrets of council

Although corruption inevitably takes over any elite secret society, the tenets put down in these triads shows that the original Druids did everything they could—at a bureaucratic level—to prevent such from happening.

The first triad example proves that "truth" and "sincerity" should be the ruling voice in Council and that social power of the Druids should be tempered with wisdom. This element is not frequently observed by ancient rulers, although we do see some evidence for it in ancient Babylon, where many of the just Kings reigned in "popularity" as opposed to "tyranny."

To possess unified strength in the Druid community is to have power—and take responsibility—to carry out whatever necessary to uphold the integrity of the Celtic world. Today we can continue this earth stewardship on the planet and in our communities with movements of ecological responsibility.

Druids exercised authority with Utilitarian elements, executing all judgments with consideration of the good of Nature and the "greater whole" in mind—the greatest good for the greatest number, including subsequent generations and the future of the planet. "The needs of the many outweigh the needs of the few, or the one..." Authentic synergy in Council can only arise form all persons being singular in their vision with the ability to carry out the goals of the organization.

Druids evolved into philosophical pacifists—they did train in combat for physical discipline but did not participate in military warfare. There are some references appearing in lore where they did bless or consecrate weapons for armies of the Celts—for example, against the Romans. Druids were neither allowed, nor did they condone in others, the ability to enact violent acts against fellow citizens. Most certainly, the Druids valued Truth above all things —as reflected in one of their most sacred axioms: Through True Knowledge, Power.

X. THE 3 RESPONSIBILITIES OF RIGHT JUDGMENT

a.) to listen openly
b.) to answer discreetly
c.) to observe mercy and justice in judgment

Responsibility for social and civic "judgment" in Keltia fell upon the Druids. Initiates of the Druid Order served the Celtic community as lawyers, physicians, teachers and government officials—all of which are positions where some "judgment" is executed regarding citizen actions. Physicians were required to listen to their patients and demonstrate appropriate bedside manner. Privileged citizen information was handled just as discreetly as we would expect from those who hold our confidence in such matters today. To understand the awesome position held by ancient Druids, you would have to imagine a top-tier organization of instruction and membership that included all leading and learned members of Celtic society—a network that would be worthy of the highest "conspiracy theories" if active today.

XI. THE 3 RIGHTS OF A BRITISH DRUID

a.) have shelter wherever they go
b.) no weapons shall be raised against them
c.) their counsel to be preferred over all others

Legends of the Druids include descriptions of their

more formal Colleges as well as solitary forest huts that individuals may have resided in temporarily, between journeys, or perhaps at the end of their physical lifetimes. Many active members of Druid community—excluding alumni holding civic positions—maintained very nomadic lifestyles dedicated to travel and the exchange of information. Bardic initiates often served as heralds, messengers, and covertly as the "eyes and ears" of the Druid Councils while out in the world-at-large. Esteemed members of the Druidic class traveled freely from village to village with the assurance that they would be well received.

Especially for many smaller towns and villages, it was an honor to be visited by Druids. They carried their teachings, music, medicine, games and wisdom with them wherever they went. In larger populated areas there might be a more permanent station of Druids and healers, but more frequently these individuals traveled to dispense their crafts as needed—and also to maintain a mobile watchful presence on the land. Therefore when rural communities were able to receive their "blessings" it was an "occasion" or "event" when they appeared. It was also assumed that they would be "put up" in the community—with shelter and food —usually provided by the noblest families in the area.

Druids were not necessarily only "priests" in the conventional sense of the word—dispersion of religion was but one of their many possible functions in Celtic society. In the ancient world, violently striking any one of them down would have been seen in the same light as we would today of an unarmed non-violent member of the clergy. Perhaps even more serious—given how high of a regard the Druids were held, it might be akin to a citizen killing a government official today.

Since the Druids had final say in all Celtic matters, public and private, the picture comes into focus. We must understand the potent presence ancient Druidism maintained in the early development of Western civilization. Though we are left with only shadows and distant echoes today, for nearly a millennium, the "weight" and "influence" of Druidic Wisdom—their counsel and judgment—was unparalleled in Europe.

XII. THE 3 INFLUENCES OF A PERSON

a.) what they believe themselves to be
b.) what others believe them to be
c.) the identity of the Self

This triad demonstrates a lesson of Druidic Psychology—the means we have to understand the personality and motivation of humans—others and ourselves. This knowledge may assist mentors in developing curriculum for students; it can assist in administering matters of state; and for personal reasons, we must always observe ourselves—our thoughts, tendencies and behaviors—to gain self-knowledge, insights that we can use to better direct the course of our own lives.

"What a person thinks they are..." regards one's self-esteem and self-image—or else "persona"—meaning essentially how you carry yourself in the world-at-large, but also thought and behavior patterns when alone. Our reality and its energy immediately interacts with our environment as we encounter the "greater world-at-large" and its systems. Even physical locations—and the people that inhabit them—have a close affinity to some type of energy or another, and this "resonance" will affect experiences and interactions that involve them.

The standards and practices, beliefs and expectations, cultural and social norms—which are uniquely in place at all times and places in history —directly affect us. It does not matter whether we wish to directly incorporate them or not, or even if we agree with them or not. In either case we are participants and we have an energetic interaction with the world around us.

We develop life experience through interactive contact with the world. In the interim, we learn to create masks, personas and facades for various situations and for different people. These masks are a glamour and not generally representative of who we truly are, yet some people become attached to them nonetheless and eventually over-identify with and assimilate these personas as "Self." Those who spend the majority of their lifetime involved with social interaction outside of Self-Honesty run this risk.

XIII. THE 3 ASPECTS TO ALWAYS KEEP IN CHECK

a.) the hand
b.) the tongue
c.) desire

What you do, what you say and how you feel are often the result of thoughts that seem to come unbidden—or from outside of us. Druidic thought discipline and willpower exercises all centered around one point: "self-control" or "self-mastery."

XIV. THE 3 AVENUES OF ACTIVE IMAGINA-TION

a.) the way things might be
b.) the way things ought to be
c.) the way things seem to be

A variation of this triad teaching may also be found as "The 3 Aspects of Wondering Left to the Imagination." This psychological lesson relates to us the nature of intellectual creativity. The Bardic grade celebrated all forms of personal artistic expression—this simple list outlined the most basic themes by which those expressions are inspired and/or interpreted.

XV. THE 3 ASPECTS AVOIDED BY THE WISE

a.) fearing the inevitable
b.) expecting the impossible
c.) grieving the irretrievable

Druid psychologists realized the sources of most pain and suffering came from within and are manifested or internalized as "stress," usually from an unnecessary source. We are not here speaking of pain from physical wounds that may be inflicted, as this is not the type of pain—unless chronic— that we carry with us throughout this life, and sometimes into the next. It is akin to what the Eastern or Buddhist traditions view as "suffering brought on by desire."

The world-at-large is based on a *systemology* that some look at as *game theory*. Without a proper understanding of how these "things" work and their holistic "place" in existence, people are likely to get themselves "worked up" over non-existent problems—misunderstood game conditions—that we are not properly educated toward in traditional societal instruction. Therefore, society becomes a mass or "Multitude" with a general inability to manage "stress" (or game conditions) to the extend that it manifests psychosomatically in the physical, emotional, mental and spiritual health of the entire community—a maze of illnesses, ailments and obstacles.

This triad demonstrates the holistic ideal of "serenity," the point where we understand that this moment *is* what it *is* as a result of all causal cosmic consequences leading to it. We are not to stress about what is likely to happen; not to expect for what is not to be in the now; or ceaselessly fret over the things we cannot change. We must be clear in our vision of how all of the parts play out a grand "game" of events and consequences—for without knowing this Cosmic Law is in effect, we could not place a sure foot forward to manifest the changes in this moment that will become apparent in the next. We are not victims or bystanders of the process—we are very much active participants. As such we must be logical and avoid the debilitating "stresses" by discovering the sequences, patterns and programs that produce these triggers and then alter the way we interact with them. It seems commonsense for organisms to discontinue behaviors that result in negative consequences, but clearly this is not always the case, and there are times where we must work to "break the pattern" to move forward.

XVI. THE 3 WAYS BY WHICH A PERSON IS MEASURED

a.) by their hopes and ideals
b.) by their fears and issues
c.) by their neutrality and indifference

The term "measured" is not meant to denote competition, but rather continues previous ideals present in "Druidic Psychology," where our goal is to understand the human condition with almost quantitative accuracy. Of course, in this triad, we are not given any numeric values for possible variables, and so this must be taken for "conceptual" use only.

In the first part, we are told "hopes and ideals"—which is also listed as "goals and ideals" or even "gods" in some versions—are significant when determining what a person strives for or models after; their "crown." This is also an indicator of what they value in the world—and about life and existence. Do they model after, aspire to and prize intellectual bookish pursuits, or raw strength and warrior-like valor? Goals, beliefs, ideals, hopes and even "gods" sacred to an individual are likely to reflect a holistic picture of their general "personality."

"Fears and issues" are the lesson challenges of this lifetime that we are meant to overcome. They are chosen—dictated by the consequence of decisions made in combination with interaction with the environment and its resources, culture, &tc. It is generally assumed that we can predict how the human condition will respond in the face of adversity based on the first part of the triad. Will a person try to think their way through or apply brute force? While it seems such things should be taken on a "case-by-case" basis, a person generally develops and carries "response mechanisms" that become automatic patterns of thought and behavior. Some translations offer this part of the triad as "demons and fears," which contemporary language could equate with "baggage," or else the "personal issues" we tend to carry with us and which serves no evolutionary purpose for us as seek to ascend on the Path. Some of these things are lessons, but they should not become weights.

XVII. THE 3 DISTRACTIONS LADEN WITH TROUBLE

a.) hunting
b.) war
c.) love for a woman

This triad does not appear as an exceptionally "deep spiritual" teaching on the surface, although it does offer a glimpse into the ancient Druidic attitude regarding visible patterns resulting from such things; and we should expect to see some kind of list, such as this, among the codes of our most archetypal class of "Nature Priests." In this spirit, we again see similarity with some of the Eastern philosophies carried by "monks."

Naturally, the Druids were lovers of all Life--they did not find acts of killing and warfare to be celebrated or worthy of praise among the masses. They intervened among the warring Celtic tribes quite frequently, which all shared stories and legends of heroes that were mighty warriors. This increased as the Celts experienced progressively more devastating encounters with the Romans, which by that time, wars were no longer civil and among tribes, but against a foreign nation that sought nothing short of a total Celtic Druid cultural and genetic annihilation.

XVIII. THE 3 ASPECTS BEYOND SOCIETAL CONTROL

a.) time
b.) space
c.) truth

In another version, this triad is presented as "The 3 Absolutes Which Appear Relative in the Physical World." This could even suggest that Druid philosophy carried at least a conceptual understanding of "space-time relativity." In the alternate versions, the three aspects are rendered: absolute time, absolute space and absolute truth. So, then, what is an *absolute*?

ABSOLUTE—implies an apartness; separation; independence; self-existence; self-sufficiency; supreme; unfettered; free.

At our highest level of understanding, the only "Absolute" is the "Law"—the "Cosmic Law"—existing beyond Time and beyond Space, and beyond all fluid change, and is therefore Above all other laws and principles. "Time and Space belong to the Infinite Nothingness, which is subject to the Absolute Law."

For those residing in the realm of Abred, the "Absolute" is the "real" hidden behind the glamour and illusion of perception. If you were to take the concept of "time" and shred it of all the subjective human misconceptions about it, you would be left with "absolute time" and find yourself in a "higher spatial dimension." Then, if you are to take all you know of spatial physics and rid them of all the misconceptions that apply only to the "physical" range of normal human perception, you are left with "absolute space" and glean a knowledge of a greater wider encompassing entangled existence where the very code of Absolute Law dictates everything that takes place across all possible levels of existence and understanding.

XIX. THE 3 FOUNDATIONS OF INNOVATION

a.) bold design
b.) frequent practice

c.) frequent mistakes

Human civilization has evolved beyond the first stages of its primitive survival—mainly reduced to water, food, shelter and clothing. This afforded other advancements and innovations through observation and critical thinking.

True innovations that propel society forward are results of high minds and independence—not the products of the "Multitudes" or popular opinions. Whether charting movements of the heavens or the exquisite artist holding the brush against canvas, bold design and innovation is not in the hands of the mediocre. This triad lends further to our understanding of the Druidic "scientific method"—one makes a "hypothesis," tests the "hypothesis," sees what works and doesn't, then re-investigates the original "hypothesis," and revises it—or not.

XX. THE 3 CAUSES OF REINCARNATION ON ABRED

a.) failure to obtain wisdom
b.) failure to attain independence
c.) failure to separate from the lower self

Alternate translations of this triad present it as: "The 3 Things That Make Rebirth Necessary for a Person" and in others, "3 Causes of Spiritual Stagnation." In essence, these are the reasons that we do not "grow" and "evolve" along the Path as part of the individual spiritual destiny hidden beneath our human experience and waiting to unfold. These are the real underlying reasons we get "frustrated" in our lives—and the reasons we invite unnecessary stress into our lives. We could go as far to say they are the underlying cause of even most physical ailments that attack the unbalanced and overstressed body.

XXI. THE 3 GRAND PURPOSES OF MATERIAL LIFE

a.) to attain happiness
b.) to spread positivity
c.) to manifest positive innovation in the world

This triad should require no additional explanation...

COMMUNICATION AND PERSUASION

The "magic of language" was prevalent throughout the Bardic grade of poetic verse and historical preservation—similar to the "scribe-priests" of Babylon, at the inception of the refined stylus-based *cuneiform* literary tradition. In Keltia, the Druids were the foremost exponent language and semantics experts. Classical accounts even refer to the powerful "Druid Voice" as a "tool" of social change, manipulation and persuasion.

Firstly—communication can be most simply defined as the relay of information, data or energy between a "sender" and a "receiver." A sender must be using clear syntax and semantic language to properly relay the message—information, data, &tc.—in a way that can be received or understood as intended. The receiver must be in an open condition to receive anything and must share the same syntax, language and mutual understanding for actual communication to exist. For persuasion, it is usually best if the receiver is also in a comfortable and perceptibly safe environment to maintain this "open" condition.

Effective communication is an exchange—not an authoritative lecture or dictation of information. Persuasion is not simply a method of manipulation toward one's own ideas. Basic tenets of persuasion may also be found at the core of the most effective educational techniques—both of which rely strongly on communication skills. Very intelligent people can be poor instructors of others without these skills, just as many great minds are also thwarted by the inability to adequately persuade or motivate others to support their ideas. Certainly this was a very important aspect of maintaining ancient Druidism.

During effective "direct communication"—involving personal interaction or close proximity—the sender should be watching for a relay of feedback or "comprehension" cues from the receiver. This completes a "communication loop" whereby the sender is able to actively respond. A projection of sound easily becomes noise when it is not understood. Communication is not taking place without a proper relay of "meaning"—even if that "meaning" is not exchanged exactly as intended. In this case we may be "misunderstanding a communication." If this is not corrected immediately, the chances are high that the gap between an "intended meaning" and "perceived meaning" will continue to grow throughout the exchange.

According to legends, Druids once possessed abilities to use sound, speech, voice and even music to directly affect moods beliefs and basic thought patterns of everyday Celtic life. We identify closely with some of these elements as nostalgia in certain modern revival fairs or reconstructionist festivals portraying the distant past. These experiences are marked by a very definitive energy signature present in the infrastructure and methods of communicable delivery. It is for these reasons that it carries a high value appeal for a certain type of person.

Persuasion is the communicative language art of affecting (altering) one's salient (surface) beliefs about some factor—even preliminary instruction regarding some matter. We are all subject to persuasion—including the very meaning prescribed to words. Obviously, effective communication skills are a prerequisite for effective persuasion. The intensity of persuasion is also relative to the comprehension level of the participant and their receipt of influential messages. Therefore, a person is unable to be truly persuaded regarding something that they don't understand—they can only be persuaded about something they understand or believe that they understand—even if it is a false understanding. The receiver must be able to understand, comprehend and elaborate the beliefs (or data) for themselves internally for a "belief" to generate. True beliefs are thoughts that we also attach emotional significance to.

Messages, data and beliefs are most effectively relayed when the "receiver" can maintain some emotional involvement with the information. We generally do not carry strong feelings or beliefs about things we find inconsequential or nonsense. The intensity of programming maintained, long after the original stimuli or impression is made, is attached to the intensity of emotional encoding or "imprinting." In short: a persuasive message must be shown to be critically relevant.

Although the actual methods of persuasion and processing are not fully agreed upon in modern clinical and academic fields of psychology, we can conclusively find evidence to support that: the knowledge base and beliefs of an individual share a direct relationship with their behaviors. Once dominated by philosophical pursuits of the "mind," it is clear that our more modern understanding of psychology is heavily dependent on "behaviorist schools" or those fields that emphasize study of the overt mechanical behaviors, patterns and sequences that outwardly may reflect aspects of internal processing, perceptions and programming. It is logical to assume that behavior can be influenced through belief-persuasion.

Humans tend to look to social norms as an indicator or benchmark of the standards they should follow; what they should believe; how they should behave. When one is unsure about something—for example, experiencing a new life stimulus—there is an almost natural or socially programmed tende-

ncy to look to others for validation—validating
our experiences from what we have learned from
others and theirs. This is how we base how we
should feel—and we will either accept what we
are given by our peers; request additional information; or spend a great deal of our attention observing the behaviors of others. The human mind
is programmed to do this in order to form the most
complete assessment—even if inaccurate—for in-
clusion in a mental slot that stores experiential
knowledge of a particular stimulus. The mind fills
in gaps of information unconsciously just to be
certain that we always "believe" we have the most
accurate, complete and clear picture of it all.

The ability for the mind to be "conditioned" or
"programmed" is a preexisting quality of the mind
—its "software" or function to receive and process
information about the external world. Most information we receive is the product of stimu-
lus-and- response, based on our experiences and
what we are shown of our world through interaction, instruction and examples. We tend to "associate" familiar things with unfamiliar, categorizing
and grouping what we "know" into "schemas"
about any and all subjects. Knowledge earned concerning macrocosmic—or "outside"—events will
contribute to facts and data we keep about "things"
and what we believe about them. We believe that
"if p then q" about every instance where knowledge is rooted in either our observations or assu-

mptions—and our emotional and mental stability seems tethered to the notion that whatever piece of the mystery we do hold and understand must be sufficient for us to survive this lifetime.

Any individual is generally able to get along in a physical life successfully without the "higher learning" associated with the "mental sciences" or "esoteric arts." A person doesn't know what they don't know until they *know*—and then they cannot not *know*. And for most people, there is nothing "more" to be known "out there"—sure, there are "things" to be seen and "labels" we give to these "new discoveries," but for a person who is not trained to "see" or for a person who has gotten on through many of their years "just fine" without *knowing*—the rest is inconsequential nonsense. And when its consequences do affect them, it is attributed to something else. Some false "*p-q*" relationship that seems to fit for their level of knowing.

We learn and develop false associations about our world all of the time. Again, most of this is rooted in stimulus-and-response—the experience of *gains* or *losses* in "game conditions" —when we *act* and then *re-act* based on perceived results. But our perceptions may be flawed, as we see in clinical studies of "classical conditioning." In a textbook example of Little Albert—a baby was repeatedly introduced to a bunny simultaneous with a loud frightening noise. The fear generated by the noise was conditionally displaced onto the bunny, resulting in a lifetime fear of bunnies. We might later call this an "irrational fear," but it is very real to the person and rationalized within the "software programming" that they are running. As a result we can associate a "Thing" to have a positive or negative reaction—or to carry a different meaning altogether—simply by repeatedly introducing it alongside blatant forms of the desired result until the response is programmed—*automatic*.

The human condition carries another tendency—one that the ongoing civilized progression of humanity is entirely dependent on—and that is "compliance." It is an unusual program at play in the mind—one that is proven to be evolutionary to our survival, and therefore deeply ingrained. Life learns very early that *rewards* and *gains* are the result of being "agreeable." This means understanding the rules and playing field and agreeing to be a participant—beyond simply learning from "social cues" we are now choosing to *play the game*. And as they say—*you can't win if you don't play*—and many unsuccessful people spend considerable energy avoiding the *game* altogether, rather than learning how to play.

As innovators, humans are also more willing to do something, or put forth their energy toward something, if it seems like it was their own idea—has originated within their own psyche. Yet, no one wants to "appear wrong," so it takes a bold personality to plunge ahead—and sometimes we are not always given the "credit" due. All of these factors are energetically relevant—whether dealing with financial investments or socially motivating the human population. Certainly we can see elements of this knowledge—and these tactics—present today in civic systems and general politics, to no less extent than perhaps they appeared in ancient times.

Programming present within the human condition is very old and very powerful. Although we have long since rejected the outer structure and terminology of "slavery" for obvious reasons, it is still present, greatly disguised, yet in plain sight.

The type of "magical presence" that earned ancient Druids their place in our memory must be a result of their higher understanding of the human condition. A higher level of understanding—an advanced experiential knowledge base—led to further success in all endeavors, activities and social roles maintained by members of this class in ancient Celtic society. These initiates were culled to focus their arts toward motivating people into peaceful prosperous living traditions—preserving a language and culture that affected the entire population and our surviving customs today: from "Christmas Trees" to "Jack-o'-lanterns."

KEYS TO
ELEMENTAL POWER

Lore of the "Natural Elements"—sometimes called *Elementalism*—may be found at the heart of nearly all modern "magical" revivals of ancient esoteric mysticism. It is certainly a paramount theme in "natural" traditions—oriented to Earth magic or "Nature." We even find evidence of this elemental model of understanding the Universe all throughout the cosmos, but it is easiest for us to assimilate the *systemology* into our daily understanding and practices when it relates specifically to the world we can see and touch—and of which we are immediately immersed in. But, all of these forces are interconnected, forming the basis of energetic relationships and interactions taking place at all levels of existence simultaneously in the cosmos.

Druids attributed qualities of the elements into a "mystical" and "magical" paradigm—but this fundamental knowledge is no more "supernatural" than the laws and tables of elements in "Chemistry"—so named for its origins in the "dark arts." It is this understanding of the natural world that provides us our storehouse of physical and metaphysical knowledge—a basis to build our interactive understanding of "how things work" and "what we can do" to cause a desired result. This alchemical combination of forces and elements is the same that fuels creation—the same processes and Cosmic Laws that are in effect with or without our belief and participation. Its study and theories about our potential participation have gone by many names throughout time. Today, we use our understanding of energetic variables—as they relate to the "Four Elements"—to conduct "magical work" that promotes Druid values and our ascent on the Path of Ascension.

The universe is a "singularity"—there is no separation. Yet, in our manifest world of infinite parts, we can find an infinite number of connections. We can begin with a twofold dualism, working our way through a threefold triad or a fourfold quadrology... in fact, for as many ways as we can divide wholeness, we can find a way to make the paradigm work. The mind is amazing in its ability to separate, fix labels and categorize a myriad of parts. For our purposes, most ancient non-chemical paradigms involving "Elementalism" relay the model best as a four-fold division of basic elements: Earth, Air, Fire and Water.

A basic four-fold elemental model is preferred by most practitioners, regardless of the tradition involved. It is popular in the Western Magical Tradition because it follows natural symmetry and cycles we easily identify in Nature; it easily pairs with the "four corners" of the World—meaning four cardinal directions—and likewise the corners, sides or quadrangles of a ceremonial temple or ritual circle. Material elements—earth and air—divide the basic essence of creation into solids and gases. Later "scientific" classifications determined liquid—or water—to be a composite of various additional elements, and fire was eventually rejected from the elemental model as a "combustion process" of elemental transformation, but not an elemental component in itself. But—that is what conventional scientific vocabulary semantics have to say about it.

In the current author's personal model,[*] earth and air correspond to the first two (primary) forms of manifestation that modern science is familiar with: gravity (G) and electromagnetism (EM). Discovery of the other two subatomic nuclear forces completes the fourfold "standard model" of Western Elementalism. In this system, fire corresponds to the weak nuclear (W) force responsible for radiation, fusion and heat. The qualities from the water element best correspond to the strong nuclear (S) force that bonds and unites particles together all across the fabric of space or sea of Infinity.

"Elementalism"—its study and implementation— is an integral part of the Druid Path. In order to fully appreciate the symphony of energies at play

---

[*] First outlined in the 2008 edition of *"Arcanum: The Great Magical Arcanum"* by Joshua Free.

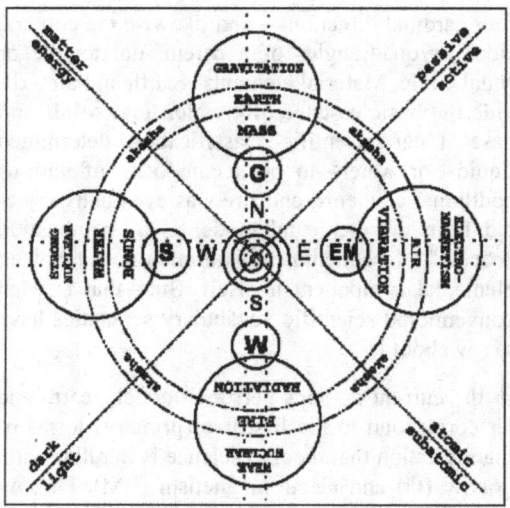

in the Universe, the seeker must also learn to perceive the elemental forces as something more than just the "perceptibly physical" manifestations and forms most easily beheld. For example—Earth is more than ground and rocks; Fire is more than a candle-flame; Air is more than just wind—and so forth.

Metaphysical and esoteric lore refers to the most perfect or pure manifestations of these elemental forces as "Elemental Kingdoms," existing outside the material range that humans are aware of. These concentrations of elemental energy interact with our world—the realm of Abred—but radiate from a "higher" encompassing dimension—Gwynedd, with its rays interconnected with all aspects of our visible world.

Where some authors and traditions relay elemental lore as an introductory side-note—or as simply a foundation for some other execution of practical or "ritual magic," which we will deal with in the next lesson-chapter—the Druids spent a considerable amount of their lifetime working and meditating in Nature, ultimately leading to a systematized understanding of elemental energies and their interconnectivity as it related to all aspects of life and existence.

In accordance with the "Doctrine of Authority," the greater amount of time spent having a communication of energy with a specific "Elemental Kingdom," the greater the state of "mastery" or "authority" achieved with that particular element. Integration of practical knowledge and the experience of energetic work with each of these elements becomes a matter of personal individuality—the point where a curriculum must be shaped for an initiate—but ultimately working through each of the elements, one by one, prior to any "functional" mystical or spiritual incorporation within the paradigm or tradition.

EARTH-IN-MIND TRAINING

The elemental journey begins with Earth, the most "concrete" and perhaps most "physical" of the elements. Not only does it represent the physical planet "earth," but also the "physical" or living components that embody the entire planetary earth system. The trees, stones, animals and even particulates are all earth-elemental forms. Hence: herbs, gems and totems are all significant to earth-oriented "*shamanism.*"

The Earth is our home—it is our dwelling place and our sense of foundation. Family is also representative of this current, and we speak of our lineage in terms of "trees" and "roots." The fertility and stability of the "family unit" is likened to earth, just as the abundance and growth of the "green world" of Nature is apparent in the wintertime and spring—showing that the cyclic bond of Nature continues on like a bloodline.

When we consider the "nourishing" and "fertile" qualities attached to the earth element, it seems logically that it is placed on the "passive" and "feminine" end of the spectrum. And not surprisingly, Druids consider the Earth, "Our Mother," whether as a "body" of some "primeval dragon" or as systems of a living "Mother Goddess"—the planetary ecosystem has long tradition of "feminine" attribute.

As an integral part of their "elemental tradition" to connect with earth energies, the Druids frequently gathered in large circles of stone—called a "*henge*"—or in circles of ancient trees—called a "*grove.*" These places reflected primal earth energy and the permanency attached to a living "earth memory." It more purely embodied a "temple of worship" to the "Source-of-All-Being" than any man-made religious "building" with walls that could only further the separation of our consciousness from Nature. Rather than literally "worshiping" Nature, as many mythographers and historians are misguided to suggest, the Druids revered an All-Source, but honored it in the midst of its most pure and direct manifestation: Nature. Our lives are easily enriched and re-enchanted from reconnection of our personal energies with those of Nature.

In the physical/ecological level of elemental expression, earth represents the whole of the land: its soil; plant-life; and all the living creatures that feed (or depend) on the same. In such beings, the earth current manifests as bones, muscle and skin —and any other form of organic tissue necessary to support the organism.

The ceremonial or energetic color associated with earth is green—and as such, "greener" terrains and geographies tend to possess more abiding reserves of earth energy. By this we mainly mean the

"Green World," which is best encountered in the woodlands, forests and valleys vividly marked by strong "earth tones." Consider also the grasslands. To really feel the earth below you, take off your shoes and socks and walk through some grassland. Take some time away from your day—and your studies—to just "sprawl out" on the ground, feeling the firm earth against your back. Lean up with your back against the trunk of the tree and see if you can imagine yourself as a part of the tree, extending the "root" of your being down into the same soil with strong roots stretching deep into the landscape.

Danubian legends of Druid magic make reference to the Stone of Fal—but there are many other representations of the earth-element that could easily be incorporated into ritual work and/or meditation, including stones and rocks of virtually any kind. Fields of Esoteric occult lore do exist concerning the natures and vibrations interpreted from various gem types, even sub-classifying them into further elemental categories. Any use of minerals, rocks and crystals, in general, may be tied to earth-elemental practice.

Another "earth-aligned" ritual tool—or symbol—that is popularly used in modern Druidic Tradition is called the "Druid's Foot." This is essentially synonymous, in form and implementation with the "witches pentacle." A "Druid's Foot" is usually a

The Earth Key

Threshold Keys—
  Threshold Direction: North ("*tuath*")
  Threshold Time: Midnight
  Threshold Season: Winter
  Threshold Festivals: Samhain (*Oct 31*)
                and Yule (*Dec 21*)
Ceremonial Keys—
  Colors: Green, brown and black.
  Tools & Implements: Stones, pentacle,
    salt, soil.
  Bardic Instrument: Drums
  Zodiacal Signs: Capricorn, Virgo and
    Taurus.
  Magic: Grounding, fertility, stone,
    trees, wood.
Alchemical Keys—
  Polarity: Moist, fertile, passive,
    feminine, lunar, physical.
  Field-Force: Gravity-(G)
  Essence: Stones
  Animal Essence: All four-legged.
  Plant Essence: Roots
  Metal Essence: Lead and silver.
  Gem Type: Heavy and dark.
  Sense: Touch (feeling)

flat wooden (or metal) disc painted white with a
black-lined five-pointed star stretching across the

surface. Some Druidic practitioners do not paint their wooden magical tools with anything artificial, and so a natural dye may be used. If a lighter colored wood is chosen for the disc, the star may be "burned" or carved into it.

WATER-IN-MIND TRAINING

Water is the second element introduced to the initiate—indicative of the subconscious and emotional aspects of Self. Being "fluid" means to be constantly subject to a "flowing" shift in form—or waves. As such, water is very similar to the nature of emotions, likened to a "tidal ebb and flow" of emotionally charged energy that is projected and received from the emotional "level"—or biochemical conduits—between the Self and its experience of the physical world. And notably, the earth planet surface and human being are approximately equal in their ratio of water to "earth."

When applied to mystical and ritual use—and our catalogue of affinities and elemental domains—the water-element has several main energetic divisions or polarities. There is, at first, the "emotional" connectivity of water—that which relates to love, friendship and happiness. In addition to this, there is a "subconscious" facet, which is also interwoven with what we consider our "emotional" side too—but it rules the domain of our sleep, dreams and other "nocturnal" activities. Finally, there is a definitive affinity of the lunar-feminine current to the water element, which manifests most significantly for our purpose as: fertility, healing and personal magnetism—including all aspects of "glamour" and influential "charisma."

Contrary to the popular or contemporary semantic attribute that "passive is weak," we can easily see how the standing stones and soil of the earth and the seas of water are quite "strong" in their solidity and existence; constantly adjusting their forms as needed, but maintaining nonetheless. Water is classified as a "passive" element, but it is hardly "weak"--putting the more obvious storms and tidal waves aside—even the most subtle presence of water has the ability to cut away new rivers and form canyons and badlands when given enough time. This demonstrates to the initiate that the earth and water elements are just as strong as any other. When we consider the forms of practical magic aligned to the water element—love, dreams, glamour, enchantment, &tc.—they all involve a "passive" and "gradual" play on our "emotions," our physical "senses" and our "perceptions." While certainly not as forthright as more bold and blatant exercises of force—certainly no one can dismiss the awesome power and strength that these "subtle" forces can actually have in our lives.

Psychologist Carl Jung believed that most darker aspects of "personality" were emotional in nature.

Jung did not view emotions as an "internally individual product," but as something that happens *to* you. We might experience emotions as results of "external" stimuli influencing our subconscious to initiate production of bio-chemical responses—those detectable in the physical body. Our emotions are not, themselves, pleasure or pain, although we often attach emotional states to these experiences. Because of a close energetic proximity with the earth element, emotions may carry evolutionary value, when used properly, toward our basic physical survival.

THE 3 ASPECTS COMPOSING EMOTIONAL EXPERIENCE[*]

a.) a subjective conscious experience
b.) physiological (biochemical) arousal
c.) expression of overt physical behavior

According to this logic, a "cognitive" (thinking) mind encounters an experience that is integrated into its subconscious mind. This must be strong enough to result in a physiologic state of arousal—meaning bio-elemental chemicals that are produced in the body: via blood, hormones, neurotransmitters and other fluid-like substances, mostly tied to the water element. All of these play a critical role in creating an emotional experience—both

---

[*]   This triad is of the author's design and not of ancient or Welsh origin.

the received encoded emotionally energy and resulting overt/observable (projected) actions/behaviors.

Just as we attach the earth element most logically to the Earth planet, the water element holds many physical and spiritual ties to the earth's closest celestial body—the *Moon*. Influence of the moon toward the gravity and tides of the waters is long known and recognized. These tidal phases are linked to the phases of the moon—for which we name our "months." There is an obvious relationship between these thirteen "moons" or "months" of the annual solar year to feminine menstrual and fertility cycles—furthering the sexual polarity of this element.

Mirrors, seashells, cauldrons, goblets, bowls, and even direct presence of "water" itself, may all be incorporated into rituals or "ceremonial" observance, representing the water energetic current. Some Druidic traditions represent the water-element with a "shell-chalice"—used to hold water and other libations during ritual operations. We find in references to "sprinkling of lustral waters" from a goblet in contemporary practices of both "high ceremonial magic" and "low magical spellcraft."

Personal insights and visions may be produced internally via the subconscious and divined through the use or assistance of some "medium" or "catalyst" aligned to the water element.

Water and mirrors—being so closely connected to the subconscious—are important mediums for "skrying"--the divination practice of "gazing." When a practitioner does such, they are not really looking *at* or *into* the selected tool—they are using the tool as a "catalyst" to consciously "open up" subconscious channels of awareness—and bring them to conscious awareness. In spite of the physical apparatus, this is all an "internal" process. It very well may be the case that nothing is objectively displayed on the water surface or skrying medium—or that the visible phenomenon will not necessarily be the same as what a *seer* is experiencing from their Mind's Eye.

When a mystic or *seer* consciously awakens the subconscious mind in the manner we have described, we call it a "trance." There are no specific ancient rules for how to "*skrye*" or enter trancelike states, although each segment of culture throughout the earth has developed their own methodologies—be it: dramatic reenactments, drumming, incense, lighting, the use of psychotropic pharmacology... any and all of which may contribute to the certain personal states or mental frequency that promotes *mystical* experience. No images or visions are "forced" or "conjured." To be effective we must maintain a clear and open channel within the mind—and wait to see what presents itself. For modern practice: try focusing on a specific question—or situation you are facing —in your mind before spending some time before a skrying medium, releasing the question from your mind—and into the medium—and thereby clearing it from your thoughts. See if anything comes to you while meditating in your "trance state." Sometimes even the simple act of releasing our hold on the "thoughts" we seek to control is what makes room for the *real magic* to happen!

Water frequently appears in magical rituals and re-ligious rites—ancient and modern—having been "blessed" or "charged" by a priest, magician or shaman. Water is unique in its ability to carry a "charge" or "intention." It may be "charged" or "magnetized" for easy storage and dispersal of any energy—and it seems most potent and receptive nearest its freezing point.

As a practical exercise, try this: whenever you wash your body with water, acknowledge the puri-fying and healing qualities inherent in the elemental substance. Envision it as possessing blessed qualities capable of washing away the iniquity of your total being—physically, emotion-ally, mentally and spiritually. When you shower— feel and see all of the negativity that has attached itself to you—and your "auric shell"—running down and off your body into the drain and out into the universal sea to be recycled, renewed and re-formed. Recent studies by Eastern scientists have even demonstrated how water can easily be charged with an intention—photographing patterns of the molecular crystals that form as result of the vibrations inherent in the intentions. This means that intentions that carry a high emotional charge can actually affect us at a very physical molecular level of our physical being!

Contact with the water-element is obviously accessible near places where water is physically present—lakes, rivers, waterfalls and even wells. Each aquatic terrain type also carries it own flavor of energetic resonance or attributes. For example: the energetic expression emanated from a turbulent river or waterfall is significantly different from what you will find at a still pond or lake.

At times of emotional stress and discord—times when one is hoping to sort out a convoluted orchestra of emotions taking place within them—humans are often drawn to places of tranquility in Nature—just as often the water-element is somehow involved. When feeling in danger, or when the need arises to release dangerous or interfering negative energy, the Druids would meditate near water—even crossing over it, such as on bridges, when possible. The ability to visualize the source of one's stress being left on the "other shore" or "behind us" or "washed away" can have real emot-

The Water Key

Threshold Keys—
   Threshold Direction: West ("*iar*")
   Threshold Time: Dusk (sunset)
   Threshold Season: Autumn
   Threshold Festivals: Lughnassadh
      (*Aug. 1*) and Autumn Equinox
      (*Sept. 21*)
Ceremonial Keys—
   Colors: Blue and silver.
   Tools & Implements: Goblet, shells
      and mirror.
   Bardic Instruments: Harp, dulcimer
      and stringed.
   Zodiacal Signs: Cancer, Scorpio and
      Pisces.
   Magic: Love, healing, fertility and
      happiness.
Alchemical Keys—
   Polarity: Wet, cold, passive, female
      and lunar.
   Field-Force: Strong-(S) Nuclear
   Essence: Metals
   Animal Essence: Marine and sea life.
   Plant Essence: Leaves
   Metal Essence: Quicksilver
   Gem Type: Clean and clear.
   Senses: Taste and intuition.

ional and psychological effects. Even better, if one can step across a river (or similar) on rocks—a pathway of rocks or leaping from stone to stone. A person can visualize themselves as overcoming a new challenge and/or barrier with each stepping stone achieved.

Spells and rituals for love and romance are the most prominent contemporary "New Age" uses of the water element. As a practical suggestion: the practitioner performing a love spell should first connect with the energetic current of water. The initiate should then combine energies from both the element of water—for love and the emotional aspect—and the fire element—to represent passion and the sexual aspect.

AIR-IN-MIND TRAINING

Consider for a moment what the "air element" means to you. At first, you might be thinking about wind or even oxygen—but think deeper. Put this book down for a moment and just take a look around you... You are going to see physical manifestations and objects as you might expect, but what of the invisible space between your eye and the objects? Have you ever stopped to consider the various "waves" of crisscrossing energy that overlapping and projecting in the space around you—and even through you?

Air is a "psychological," "mental" or "intellectual" element, and the first of the "active" ones on our journey. Once an initiate has encountered—and mastered—the "physical" (*earth*) and "emotional" (*water*) aspects of Self—they are led to the air element to experience the faculties of the "mind." The actual energy frequency—or vibration—at the "mental" level of Self is at a relatively higher rate than we find with the "emotional" realm (*water*), which is itself slightly higher than the "earth" or condensed "physical" realm.

Thought discipline, willpower and visualization are all aspects of the air element. Ritual magic and other practical workings employ all of these facets to be effective—Such magic usually operates from the "mental level" in order to influence (affect) the emotional-physical realms of mundane experience and perception. Whenever you want to change something—whether physical or metaphysical—you must first "visualize" the effect as though it has already happened, in its entirety or a state of completion. This is a fundamental mental practice in order to achieve the clearest "picture" in the mind—the model or image that we use as our focus to direct our goal-seeking energies and attention. This correlates directly with an ancient esoteric teaching: *action follows thought*.

Air is the element of communication—with an energetic affinity for the respiratory system, breath, voice and sound—the formation of wave patterns that carry the energy of the other elements. Divination practices—such as the use of an oracle—are also governed by the air element, as a "communication" between the "seen" and "unseen" realms.

In ritual magic, and other similar applications throughout history, the air element is attributed to the mind—the mental or psychological level of existence and processing—the archetypal domain of the Druid or "wizard." As such, the element, and its representation of the "active mind" in ritual, is best represented by the "wand"—equally iconic in consciousness when we conjure images of magicians and witches. The wand is symbolic of intellectual power and prowess of the "magic-user"— and their ability to channel (direct) the energetic currents of the cosmos, as interconnected with the mind. Wands then becomes a "focusing" tool for associated elemental energies—much like other "ritual implements" found in the occult.

In contemporary Druidic lore, wands are cut from branches of specifically selected trees in the light of a full moon—and they are not to have touched the ground. As an air tool, many practitioners have difficulties in using a piece of fallen wood taken from the ground to craft such a sacred object. Certainly there are other instances where such is acceptable or even preferred, but some lore strongly suggests that the time, season, place and type of

The Air Key

Threshold Keys—
   Threshold Direction: East ("*aiet*")
   Threshold Time: Dawn (sunrise)
   Threshold Season: Spring
   Threshold Festivals: Imbolc (*Feb. 1*)
    and Spring Equinox (*March 21*)

Ceremonial Keys—
   Colors: Yellow and purple.
   Tools & Implements: Wand, incense,
    feathers.
   Bardic Instruments: Chimes, flutes
    and wind.
   Zodiacal Signs: Gemini, Libra and
    Aquarius.
   Magic: Visualization, discipline and
    divination.

Alchemical Keys—
   Polarity: Dry, expansive, active and
    masculine.
   Field-Force: Electromagnetism-(EM)
   Essence: Plants and flowers.
   Animal Essence: Birds and winged.
   Plant Essence: Flowers
   Metal Essence: Copper and tin.
   Gem Type: Light and crystalline.
   Sense: Hearing and smell.

tree that the wood is collected from will all have an energetic effect on the wand-tool itself—and using the "elemental keys," a person might ascertain what these additional properties might be. Be sure to keep in mind: Druids always "ask" trees for permission before removing anything from them. This is a long-standing practice of mutual respect between Druids and the natural world.

Traditionally, the Druidic wand is fashioned from *oak* wood— though *ash* also seems to have played a key role in some Celtic traditions. The air-wand is based, at least in part, on the *Spear of Lugh*— made of ash—appearing in Danubian Druid legends. As a result, the Celts commonly used ash wood to fashion their spears, so it is not surprising to see so many references to ash-wands. Of course, many other types of tree may be potentially used as wand-wood, though it is suggested to do research into the energies attached to different tree types before doing so.

Personal and "magical" energy is projected (and sent out) to whatever focus we give our conscious attention to. This corresponds well with the esoteric axiom: *energy flows where attention goes*. Mental discipline and the ability to concentrate are critical to magical success. Just as you must visualize, plan and execute action toward any change seen in the Mind's Eye, so too must "magical rituals" be practiced—following the same steps, even if direct "physical action" is not what is being applied during a "spell-like" working, rite or meditation.

FIRE-IN-MIND TRAINING

The technological evolution of humanity began with mastery—and use—of *fire*. Of all the elements, *fire* has the most active vibration—the second current of "manifestation" (after *air*). It possesses no "passive" qualities. A raging fire current creates change swiftly in comparison to other elemental transformations. Without temperance and wisdom, the destructive side of *fire* can become uncontrollable. As such, the intensity of the current is sharp and quick but must be continually fed to keep it alive—though it is generally only briefly needed, since its sweeping effects linger long after the flames have died down.

Our journey on the "Elemental Path," brings us to the fire element last—the element representing the highest vibrations of the physical world as linked to the highest spiritual manifestations. Where the earth is connected to our physical form; the waters to our emotions; and the air to the mind—the fires are symbolically linked to our spiritual form, that burning spirit taking residence within the other forms—the spirit that is the "I AM"—or true *Self* —that is doing the experiencing by its connection to these other "levels" of existence.

In practical magic, rituals and ceremonies, the fire element is most frequently represented by a "bladed" object—a sword or dagger, or a representation thereof. Newer Wiccan traditions use the term "athame" (*ah-thay-may*) for their black handled ritual blade—used to trace boundaries of the ritual circle, and various signs in the air when in place of a wand. Druids also used a white-handled or bone-handled "boline" blade exclusively for cutting sacred herbs. One legendary example of an ancient Druidic "fire-boline" is the "golden sickle."

Another fire-oriented tool popularly associated with Druids and wizards: the staff. They are similar to wands except they do not channel and direct energy as quickly for immediate use, but instead gradually develop a strong "charge" for eventual use. These fire tools—like the "sword" and "staff"—are often given a unique personal "name" by their owners, and as such they develop a personality over time. They may become powerful magical artifacts with enough time and use—as is possible with all other ritual tools—to carry a magical charge long after the original lifetime of its possessor.

As an intermediary between our true spiritual Self and the mental, emotional and physical degrees of our chosen Identity, the fire element represents the Will—the power of the Self to execute control

The Fire Key

Threshold Keys—
  Threshold Direction: South ('*deas*')
  Threshold Time: Noon
  Threshold Season: Summer
  Threshold Festival: Beltane (*May 1*)
          and Summer Solstice (*June 21*)
Ceremonial Keys—
  Colors: Red, orange, white and gold
  Tools & Implements: Sword, sickle,
    blade, staff, candles and actual fire.
  Bardic Instruments: Trumpets, horns
    and brass.
  Zodiacal Signs: Aries, Leo and
    Sagittarius.
  Magic: Alchemy, transformation and
    sex magic.
Alchemical Keys—
  Polarity: Dry, heat, expansive,
    masculine, solar.
  Field-Force: Weak-(N) Nuclear
  Essence: Animals
  Animal Essence: Lizards and reptiles.
  Plant Essence: Seeds
  Metal Essence: Gold and iron.
  Gem Type: Bright
  Sense: Sight

over all other expressions of our Self. Just as the "wand" or air-element reflects the Druid's mastery over "mind," so too is a fire-elemental sword or staff symbolic of the spiritual "willpower" and effective ability to direct its energies. Willpower and concentration may be strengthened with proper use of visualization and self-control. Remember: to be a master of the universe first requires self-mastery!

In Nature, the fire current is found clearest in the desert, and when combined with the air element: in lightning and electricity. It is also present during wildfires, geographic badlands, active volcanoes and volcanically formed mountains. When combined vigorously with the earth element, fire manifests as earthquakes. Conventional physics notes similar transformative activity as the power laden in fusion, alchemy (chemistry) and all nuclear reactions.

Candles are often used in ritual and meditation to represent the fire element. In traditional "spellcraft," candles can even represent a particular person, place or idea. They are lit with specific intentions in mind—sometimes correlated with verbal affirmations of intent (e.g. the "spell"). Mostly, the candle acts as a focal device, permitting "magic-users" to direct (channel) energy to the target (associated with the representation).

ELEMENTS OF DRUID RITUAL

The primary elements of Druid ritualcraft are as follows:

---

1. Earth Phase
Physical preparations; the outer environment; personal grounding; meditation; and phsyical preparation of the "circle"—ritual space or "nemeton."

2. Water Phase
Inner preparations; internal set and focus; the focus of intention; and "altering personal energy vibrations" to match frequencies of the energy attracted.

3. Air Phase
Internal intentions meet externals; communication via vocalization ("spell"); sound and smell (incense)—all of which represent the first step toward "manifestation."

4. Fire Phase
Visualization; reconnection to original intentions; using will-power to raise personal energy; incorporating external energies/ forces; and finally releasing the energy into the cosmos and toward the goal.

Rituals are predetermined formulas for channeling energetic currents toward a specific goal. In most practical applications, "ritual magic" is elementally oriented. Even the ritual structure itself has elemental alignments. In addition to these, the elemental forces are directly summoned with the presence of the elementally-aligned ritual tools (previously described).

EARTH PHASE

Personal Preparations: Before conducting any physical ritual, the Druid must be completely prepared—internally (whether that be your spiritual and mental set or emotional state) and externally (including everything from your physical body to any items and tools that will be incorporated).

Firstly, cleanse the body and wear clean clothing (or robes) for the ritual—cleanliness and new or freshly laundered linens will help deter outside static or disruptive energy that might otherwise be attached to mundane items. Secondly, a Druid must mentally prepare themselves prior to any ritual work. Review any relevant magical lore or related knowledge that is either related to Druidry, the elements, ritual magic, or another facet intended for ceremonial incorporation. If there are incantations to be spoken, it is best—though not necessary—to have them memorized so they are sincerely spoken fluently and with full comprehension of their meaning during the operation. Finally, all physical items that should be present for the ceremony must be gathered and placed within the "ritual work space"—also called a "nemeton."

Physical Preparation of the Circle: Once the working area is determined, all physical aspects of the "circle" (nemeton) must be considered. This prevents concentration from being broken later, as effective rituals are fluid wave-like motions of energy. Cleanse the existing (static) energy of the location. Traditionally this is easily accomplished by "sweeping" the area with a broom—an act carrying both physical and spiritual connotations. Unnecessary ruble (if outdoors) or distractions (such as wall-hangings, &tc., if inside) should be cleared from the work space. The physical boundaries of the "circle" (work area) may be defined by some object (or objects). When conducted outside, the "ritual circle," in accordance with the Druidic tradition, is often marked by a stone circle ("henge") or else, the selected ritual area is frequently a woodland clearing within a circle of trees (or "grove")—but always a "circle."

Neutralization of Existing Energies: The Druid must meditate to bring an energetic unifying harmony to the ritual space and all of its implements present—tuning the space and tools to a similar vibration or frequency, one meeting their own nature and as they relate to the goals of the ritual—essentially activating them with a conscious recognition of their "magical" qualities. To "clear," "ground," "concentrate" and "focus" energies effectively with awareness during ritual, the space must be either previously established as "sacred" or intentionally "consecrated" for Druidic purposes. This is easily accomplished with a sincere prayer or incantation to the "Spirit of the Place"—sometimes anthropomorphized as the goddess "Nemetona." This intention—or the activation of ritual space— is often more appropriately visualized or silently "willed."

The Druid now raises their awareness—or enter what is known as the "Body of Light." This is accomplished by consciously recognizing their "astral body" or "light body" and projecting personal consciousness into it—while simultaneously working the ritual from the physical body. This conscious awareness is maintained for the duration of the ritual. When the Druid has raised their own personal awareness—and they have extended that awareness outward to the boundaries of their microcosmic nemeton—then they are ready to consecrate the energetic space of the "sphere" or "nemeton" with some conscious form of ritualized *"circle casting."*

WATER PHASE

Awakening the Elemental Currents: The Druid

proceeds to "open" the ceremonial channels to the "elemental currents"—as if opening an energetic floodgate. Doing so creates a communicative link —or energy exchange—between the "nemeton" and "Elemental Kingdoms," or between seen and unseen spaces. Since each cardinal direction represents a specific element, ritual texts recognize elemental energetic currents as "coming in" to the nemeton by way of each of these directions.

Druids alert the universe about their ceremonies in several ways. Doing so provides a physical and metaphysical beacon to the cosmos that "something magical is about to happen." To aid in attracting these forces to the circle, the tool that is best aligned to each element is placed at that "quarter" of the circle—in alignment with the appropriate cardinal direction—along with a candle of an appropriate color; a lamp or bonfire.

Summoning Elemental Currents from the Quarters: As stated: each of the four elements is perceived as possessing a unique current of energy flowing from one of the four directions. Within the spectrum of visualization, these currents may be seen as bands of colored light. The Druid could, for example, fill the "nemeton sphere" with a watery-blue tranquil and peaceful energy in which to charge a "healing" ritual, and so forth.

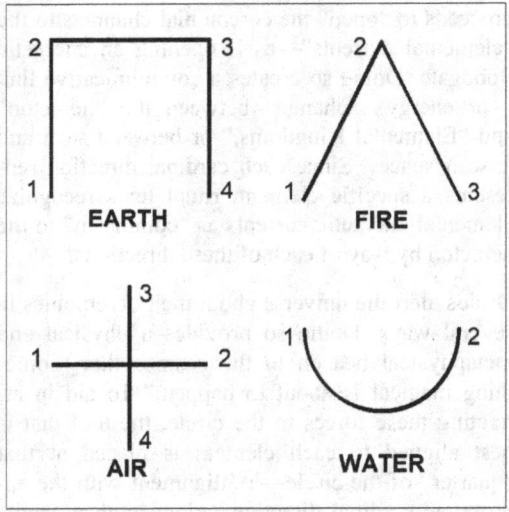

At this stage of the ritual, the Druid openly invites in the energetic presence from the Elemental Kingdoms using invocation, active visualization and intention—and with an appropriate "elemental tool," traces a sign or glyph in the air at each corresponding direction, visualized in an appropriate color.

Statement of Purpose: After having called forth external or elemental energy, the Druid makes a firm statement of intention (purpose) to inform external etheric intelligences of the intention—but also, and perhaps more importantly, to refocus their consciousness onto the actual ritual goal after

performing ceremonial preliminaries. Some esoteric lore suggests that any intention—especially
in the instance of rituals—should be stated three
times before releasing energy to it.

AIR PHASE

Expression of Intention via Catalysts: The Druid
will use various tools and implements to carry out
symbolic operations energetically linked to the
goal. For example, the Druid may light a candle of
an appropriate color representing the intention; fu-
migate the circle with an incense that is sensually
aligned to the goal; even empower or "charge" a
talisman or amulet to project energetic effects of
the ritual long after the original working has
ended.

The First Phase of Manifestation: For energy to
manifest, it must have a precise direction. The air
may have freedom of movement to blow in many
directions—and may rapidly shift at any moment
—but it is generally focused on only one direction
of travel at a time. And just as wind must choose a
specific direction to blow in, so too much the air-
aligned mind maintain the singular clarity of the
intention to be sure that our thoughts and intentions "blow" to where they need to be. The intention must be entirely clear before you direct any
energy in order to be effective—and prevent any
type of "wild magic."

Precision Awareness of the Goal: The "need" is examined to be sure it is for the "highest good." Sometimes, divination is performed to check this. Then, after the Druid is certain that the intentions are clear, they gather their own energies and combine them with the forces culled into the "pool" and prepare to fix the totality of ritually raised energy toward the goal.

FIRE PHASE

Visualizing Desired Change: The Druid fixes the goal in their mind, seeing the outcome as if it has already happened in the present—alerting the subconscious mind to operate as though this change is current. By assimilating that knowledge, the energy of this "new reality" is first interacted with internally before it is radiated out like heat from a flame.

Belief Imparts Reality: In ritual magic, visualizations are a catalyst to actually implementing physical actions. *Action follows thought.* Direct effective action comes from right thinking.

The Second Phase of Manifestation: Energetic alchemy ensues. In short: the Druid combines (or merges) internal personal stores of energy with the external energies summoned, then directs the energy as a single current—ultimately "uploading" them into the Universal consciousness; released in the cosmic mind.

Resolution: When the ritual is completed, it is customary to formally thank and dismiss any energies called to the *nemeton*, particularly representatives of the "Elemental Kingdom" or any other spirits or entities called by name. For psychological consistency, this procedure is sometimes done in reverse order—beginning with the last name called in to the ritual at the start. Likewise, elemental forces are dismissed counterclockwise, opposite of how they are called—and the energy of the circle is disbanded in equal manner.

In order to keep energies sent out by the Druid (toward the goal) from lingering or remaining attached to the ritual itself, it is best if the ceremony is not thought about after its completion. Worrying about the results and further charging the work with attention-energy will provide no positive results. Since the use of magic and concentration does consume energy and/or occupy attention, it is often advised to follow a ceremonial and meditation workings with a small meal and perhaps rest and/or sleep.

IN THE GROVE OF DRUIDS

Some scholarly discrepancies exist concerning the role and function of the "Ovate"—or "*Ovydd*" Grade of Druidry—though all mutually agree that these novitiates wore green ceremonially and participated in a curriculum that carried high affinity with the "Green World" of Nature. Most ancient sources indicate the Ovydd grade was reserved for newly initiated novices—those just beginning on their path of apprenticeship; yet, modern catalogues—those influenced by the Bardic tradition of Wales—indicate that Ovates were "Initiates of the Second Circle" and that the grade was composed of Bardic graduates. The Welsh Bardic rules for "grade" admittance is given in the appendix as "The Voice Conventional of the Bards of Britain."

Among the many "green" facets of the Ovydd curriculum we discover metaphysical and medicinal properties of trees and herbs. This immediately demonstrates a key focal difference: where the Bardic curriculum emphasized the "Elements," the Ovate grade is an intensive study of—and immersion into—the natural "growing" *Green World*. It was not uncommon during this portion of the journey for Ovate initiates to develop a particular attachment to certain locations and wilderness regions to hone their skills. In time, they may even choose to become stewards of the area—"Guardians."

The Ovate is provided with the means to commune with the Natural world in order to divine the further deepest mysteries of Druid Wisdom. Although this is always a goal of the Druid, the later lessons of apprenticeship and instruction allow for a greater amount of independent study in Nature, where a student is increasingly left to master the lessons on their own, in addition to practical skills of self-reliance and rural survival.

If we consider the modern standard division of grades—Bard, Ovate, Druid—as academic equivalents to Bachelor, Masters and Ph.D, then we would expect there to be fewer Ovates (or Initiates of the Second Circle) than Bards in Celtic society, and even fewer Druid "Initiates of the Third Circle." We should expect a majority of the Bardic apprentices (of the "First Circle") never reached the Second/Ovydd grade—itself a probationary period for students seeking entrance into the Druid Colleges later. Where the Bardic progress depended on a working understanding of Elemental Forces, progress on the Ovate path mainly relied on a growing personal relationship with physical "growing" expressions of the "Green World" of Nature—and an ability to "commune" or "connect" with the land. *Many are called; but few are chosen.*

An affinity for "Nature" is what attracts many to the Druid Path today and undoubtedly led many of the ancients into the folds, though there were those in the ranks that did not have such "Self-Honest" interests. We find elusive legends of "Dark Druids" and those who left their training early and fell to poor choices. If an Ovydd initiate could not establish the necessary link with the Earth— thereby granted direct access to blessings and teachings from Nature—then the Ovate would not be able to actually transcend or graduate the degree. Many such students would leave the "Mystery School" before their maturity to pursue their own methodology independently, contributing to many of the rural "folk traditions," that sprung up on the outskirts of the community—such as gypsies and witches.

The probationary period of the Ovydd grade is set to determine what unique relationship the Druid has with the "Green World." Such a connection cannot be synthesized. It reflects the nature of one's true Self. The Ovydd remained an "Initiate of the Second Circle" until they were able to understand—"hear" and "read"—Nature. This process allowed the leading Druids to "weed out" candidates for Druidic College admission by process of "natural selection." Only those who truly met the "call" of the Earth and were permitted to be its Guardians.

The highest degrees of Druidic curriculum continue the ideals of the Path as set forth at the beginning—to dissolve separations formed in human consciousness between the Self and Nature—or else the "Universe." Of all the representative expressions of life, it is typically the tree and plant kingdom—in addition to its animal residents—that takes precedence as the catalyst of "healing" the "Human-to-Nature relationship." As such, these key facets play the most significant role in the Ovydd curriculum of Druidic wisdom. We have realized—and hopefully soon enough—that by distancing themselves from Nature, the human race has distanced themselves—physically, emotionally, in consciousness and spirit—from the Source. It is from the human side that this gap must be bridged—for it is humanity that decided to move their focus away: The Source is Absolute —still as everywhere as it always was and will be.

Oghamology & Oghamancy

The "*Ogham*" (or "*Ogam*") alphabet is sometimes referred to as the Druidic (or Celtic) "Tree Alphabet" because of its close affinity with the "Green World" and "forest lessons" associated with the Ovydd grade curriculum. The *runic* character-letters may be used to represent a systematic catalogue of various aspects—much like the four elements have their attributes—but it is trees specifically that most obviously stand apart in lore.

Druids exclusively used the Ogham in Celtic society; it was not a "common" alphabet of the Celts themselves. Evidence of it, remaining from ancient times, is prominently found throughout Western Europe—but it is especially significant in Britain and Ireland, as once used by Druids to spread coded messages during their extensive wartime with the Romans.

Even prior to the Roman occupation of Keltia, the main function of the Ogham in Druidry was communication—including preservation of sacred lore. The standardized form of Ogham seen commonly today was established around 600 B.C. Before this time, we see many proto-Ogham examples of script—all of which are very reminiscent to the hash-styling of the original Mesopotamian writing system: proto-Sumerian cuneiform. It is very possible that early Druids possessed a similar form of quasi-cuneiform when we consider an ancient migration from the *Near East* and across the European continent. Later on, we know they employed Greek character-letters in formal writing but retained the Ogham for internal matters. Its continued use was not "primitive," since it was not the only writing system at their disposal—use of Ogham script was selected by choice.

Not unlike similar ancient systems of the Egyptians and Babylonians, the Druids attributed origins of the Ogham script to a Hermes-Thoth- Nabu-archetypal deity in their own language—named Ogma, Ogmha or Ogmos. He is adopted into the Celtic "pantheon" as the "god of writing" and a sacred patron to all Bards and Druids. In some lore, he is called "Ogma Sun-Face." *Lebor Ogaim* —or the Irish *Auraicept na n'Eces* ("The Scholar's Primer") concisely presents his lineage after administering a lesson on the Babylonian origins of language. When the master is asked: "What are the place, time, person, and cause of the invention of the Ogham?" The response is:

> "Not hard. Its place: *Hibernia insula quavi nos Scoti habitamus*. In the time of Bres, son of Elatha, King of Ireland, it was invented. Its person, Ogma, son of Elatha, son of Delbaeth, brother to Bres—for Bres, Ogma and Delbaeth are the three sons of Elatha son of Delbaeth there.

> "Now Ogma, a man well skilled in speech and in poetry, invented the Ogham. The cause of its invention: as a proof of his ingenuity, and that this speech should belong to the learned apart, to the exclusion of rustics and herdsmen.

> "When the Ogham got its name: according to sound and matter, who are the father and mother of the Ogham..."

With revival interest in Celtic matters, individual
characters of Ogham script have been transliter-
ated and understood for over a century—but it was
really the efforts of Colin Murray, and his wife
Elizabeth, that brought real public interest to the
Ogham as a "Celtic Tree Oracle" for New Age
Druidism. It has evolved in the past several decades as an intricate system of divination and runic
magic—and since the Murray's original in 1988,
there are more than just a few of these similar
"ready-made" tree magic kits appearing on the
market. Many of the modern uses and innovations
of applying correspondences to other aspects of
magical practice are not part of long-standing tradition, but they are significant in more recent
revivals.

Traditionally, in ancient times, Ogham characters
—or "fews." spelled "*fidh*" and "*fedha*" (plural)—
were cut in rock or burned into wood using a vertical axis line, "stemline" or "*droim*" and the individual hash marks are called "fleasc" or "fleasg."
The Celtic world was once littered with such posts
and road-signs, coded messages and instructions
for learned travelers—such as the location of a
nearby "grove" or "sanctuary," or a meeting place
where a convocation was held. As such, the
Ogham provided a network of discrete communication all throughout Keltia. These same letter-char-
acters could also be transmitted directly in person
as a silent form of hand signs that required point-

ing to certain knuckles and fingers—something entirely revolutionary for its time.

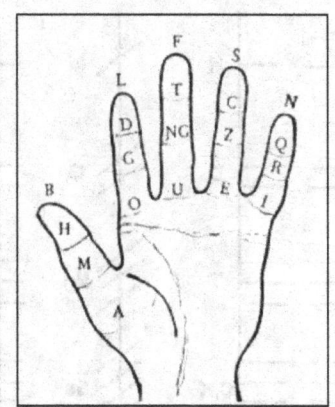

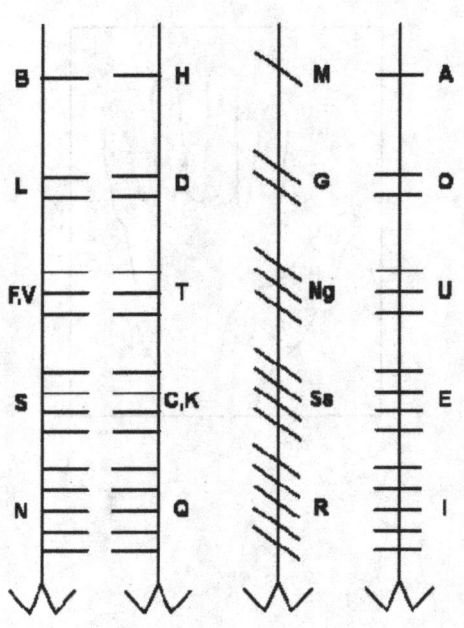

TRADITIONAL OGHAM SCALES

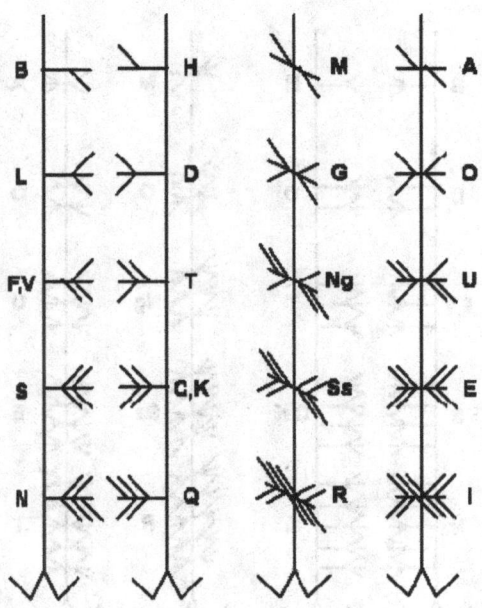

**PROGRESSIVE-BRANCH
OGHAM VARIATION**

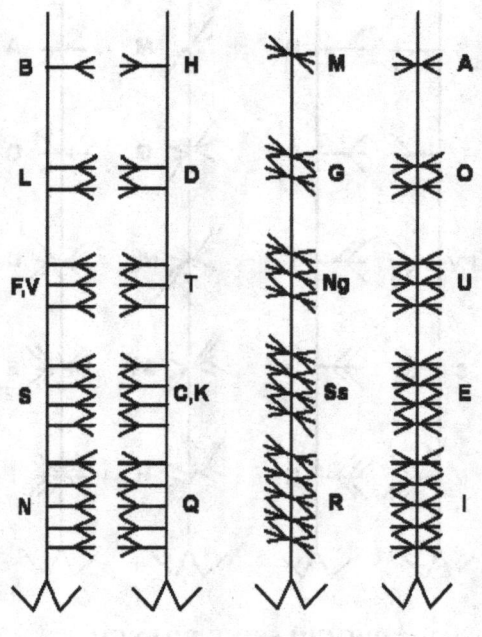

ELF-SIGN OGHAM VARIATION

As seen from our previous examples, the original Ogham alphabet is composed of twenty main characters divided into four groups of five. Each group of five is called an "*aicme*" and they are arranged phonetically.

1st *aicme* — "Labials" : B, L, F, S, N
2nd *aicme* — "Aspirants" : H, D, T, C, Q
3rd *aicme* — "Gutturals" : M, G, Ng, SS, R
4th *aicme* — "Vowels" : A, O, U, E, I

For modern purposes, the linguistic correlation between the letters given and those missing are easy to establish by applying a few simple rules. The "J" and "Y" are both Semitic mutations of "I" and therefore are all represented by the same Ogham. The "K" and "C" are also congruent. "F" and "V" have the same phonemics as does "U" and "W." Double "S" ("SS") can be used to denote "Z." Over the centuries, "new" Ogham characters ("fews") were added to the original 20, but these are of a different system and will not be discussed here.

Ogham script may been found carved into all various types of medium. Different materials also affect what the actual script is called once carved. For example—when the Ogham is carved onto wood, the script is called "*coelbren.*" If engraved in stone, then its "*coelvain.*" If Ogham is not carved, but "burned" into the wood, it is called "*cryven.*" Small Ogham "wands" used for modern practices of divination, &tc., are based on a genuine ancient set of tools called "fleasc filidh," which were kept together in what the Druid's refer to as their "Crane's Bag" for divining *Crane Knowledge*, another term for Nature's secrets. If-worn or carried, Ogham talismans are called "lly-thrau." There are several unique sets of "Ogham tools" that may be created.

Ogham Sticks. A set of sticks/twigs of the same type, cut to the same size and polished. An alternate version uses wood-chips as "runic wood-stones." Each of the sticks (or chips) will have one of the Ogham glyphs burned, carved or painted thereon. Ogham Sticks are used for high-divination and "*cryptomancy,*" or discerning "secret" names or words.

Ogham Wands. A set of wands/sticks that may range from eight to sixteen inches in length—constructed from the correlating tree type for each Ogham rune, or a tree of similar energy for any species you can't find locally represented. The "handle" of the wand should be shaved flat on one side so that you have a surface to put the Ogham few. The other end should be shaved to a stake-like or spear-like point so that it can be pushed several inches into the ground with the least effort —while the Druid holds the "handle" to complete the energetic circuit. These "Ogham Wands" are mainly used for tree communication and spiritual communion with Nature.

Ogham Rods. A set of rods used specifically for divination. They are pieces of dowel or thin wood that are cut to equal lengths, twenty-one in all. Some scholars suggest this ancient tool set is responsible for inspiring a once popular game called "pick-up-sticks," which is actually very similar to what an objective observer might see while watching a Druid cast, interpret and retrieve them. They are held in one hand about a foot away from the ground, and then dropped. Using "runic" Ogham symbolism as reference, the Druid interprets any omens able to be "read" from the "spread." Furthermore, when used in conjunction with rites of tree communication, simple acts of divination can actually become powerful workings of magic.

The "Tree Ogham" is classified as follows:

B – *beith* – birch tree
L – *luis* – rowan tree
F – *fearn* – alder tree
S – *saille* – willow tree
N – *nuin* – apple tree

H – *huatha* – hawthorn tree
D – *duir* – oak tree
T – *tinne* – holly tree
C – *coll* – hazel tree
Q – *quert* – apple tree

M – *muin* – vines
G – *gort* – ivy
Ng – *ngetal* – reed
SS – *straif* – blackthorn tree
R – *ruis* – elder tree

A – *ailim* – fir/pine tree
O – *ohn* – furze
U – *ur / uchelwydd* – mistletoe
E – *eadha* – aspen tree
I – *ioho* – yew tree

The Druid's Rod

Lore of the "Druid's Rod" is little-known among modern revivals, but this ancient tool was traditionally created and carried by an Ovydd during their work in the forests. Technically, it is *two* "rods" connected by a cord—strikingly similar to the manner nunchuka weapons are fashioned. These "Druid's Rod" had many purposes—one of which, unofficially, may very well have been self-defense.

The two rods are attached with the cord so that outstretched, there is a rod at each end with the cord between them. By fixing one portion in the ground and using the other to trace boundaries of a nemeton (or ritual circle), the Druid's Rod acts like a drawing compass. It may also be arranged to form a sun-dial. As such, uses for this tool make it a symbolic representation of cosmic knowledge, authority and practical mastery of "space-time."

The "Druid's Rod" employs another important facet of little-known Druidic lore, called the "Megalithic Yard" (abbreviated as "MY"). A "Megalithic Yard" is equivalent to 2.72 feet (which some modern practitioners simply round off to 3 feet). In "The 21 Lessons of Merlyn" by Douglas Monroe, the conversion is given as: 1 MY = 0.829 metres—equivalent to 82.9 centimeters. The complete "Druid's Rod" is composed of three measured parts—each 2.72 (or 3) feet long, making the total length approximately 9 feet , or 8.16 if using the strict "Megalithic Yard."

To be completely accurate, the Megalithic Yard is a "theoretical" system of measurement that was *probably* used in the construction of many ancient megalithic sites throught Keltia. Alexander Thom —a Scottish engineer—first discovered the Megalithic Yard. He found several ancient Celtic henges that were built with an oblong diameter of 125 MY. He also believed that the original "sacred circles" were really "ellipses," a form that more correctly follows precession of the cosmos.

ANCESTORS AND ANIMALS
—A WORLD OF TOTEMS—

When we examine the surviving legends, spiritual teachings and mystical lore attached to Druidry— and even "Celtic Mythology"—we find all manner of ethereal "astral" phenomenon within the sensory range of certain individuals and "visionaries." Therefore, there is no shortage of cultural belief in spirit guides, guardian wards, elementary being, winged messengers and ancestral family spirits— all of which are retained within "Universal Memory" and "Earth Memory" and are therefore able to be called upon, at will, by the Druid.

Certain spiritual entities—or intelligences—may come to serve as unique "guides" or "guardians" to people, places and even specific currents of energy. The energetic ties usually relate to people following in the ancestral line, or else linked by some other event—"magical" or emotionally-induced—or through regular (repeated) contact. They are most often classified as "ancestors," "faerie folk," "gods," or by even more modern semantics, "angels." Various Druid traditions—and even other systems of rural "shamanism"—believe that trees and expecially animals are imbued with an individual "spiritual self." These sentient spirits are able to manipulate energy of creation—at their own level of awareness—just as the Druid does.

These beings or forms of life are said to be assisting the Druid from the "spirit world"—or "*Gwynedd*"—which is to say the "astral plane" by contemporary standards.

"Spirit Guides" are generally considered long-term assistants that aid an individual over a period of time. This is different than a random "elemental" or even a specific "entity" that is called to the "circle" ("nemeton") to be a co-magician for the duration of a brief ritual. It is not uncommon for a "spirit guide" to shadow someone for their entire lifetime.

Celts and Druids also held ancestral spirits and ancestral—or genetic—memory in high regard; something that modern society has generally lost touch with. Many cultures believe that ancestral spirits—or at least some resonance of them—lingers around their descendents. Some even believe that stronger traits a person carried during their physical life may be amplified and called on as "powers" after passing into the "Spirit World." A Druid might call upon them for assistance by prayers and remembrance, or an specifically designed rites, asking those who have gone before them to lend their knowledge and strength. Altars and shrines might be set up to leave offerings of food before images or personal items and family heirlooms. Such is the originally observed purpose of Halloween—known to ancient Druids as the

"Feast of Ancestors" or "*Samhain.*"

Many indications are present in our everyday life to promote some belief in the presence and inter-action of spiritual entities. These experiences—their nature and intensity—are often linked to the level of awareness an individual maintains. We can only classify experience to the extent that we are capable of understanding it—leaving a wide band of the spectrum outside the boundaries of our nor-mal range of sensory input. These other impres-sions are called "subtle energies" because the de-tection from within our range is quite slight. Cer-tainly, we have all caught sight of energetic anom-alies from out the "corner of our eye," or in "dis-torted shimmering shadows," or "objects with morphing faces that appear and disappear," and the "feeling of being watched..." How many of these things do we require before we desire to raise our level of awareness?Most traditions identify active work with "Spirit Guides" as a form of "energy work"—meaning that meditation and intentional use of willpower are preferred catalysts, even over the more formalized rituals and ceremonies—such as one might derive from some "Medieval grim-oire" of spirit evocation.

In the same line as humans and their spiritual evol-ution, animals are "spiritual" beings sharing a ma-terial manifestation on the "physical plane"—or *Abred.* An incorporation of their spiritual energy,

representative traits, and other magical correspondences, is a traditional staple of most practical
systems of "natural" magic, mysticism and shamanism. "Totem animals" may be sacred due to: a
connection to ancestry; because they appear frequently in dreams; they appear frequently as personal omens in the natural/physical world; or they
are a type that an individual shares natural affinity
or kinship with. Although all animals are considered sacred expressions of life, there usually are
always a handful of specific ones uniquely attached to a person's own characteristics and personality.

Sacred animals are encountered in meditations,
visualizations and astral work—with the Otherworld or *Gwynedd*. As with "*skrying*," a Druid will
work with the "spirit" energy of an animal from a
"trance-state," possibly after activating the "Body
of Light." This same procedure is followed whether a physical animal is present or a spiritual representation of it. The ability to observe animals in
Nature—within their natural habitat—is very helpful in redeveloping this human-and-animal connection. Appreciation for animal-life in general
prerequisite for the Druid Path—as is an appreciation of all life.

Work with ethereal spirits, ancestors and Spirit
Guides is often conducted on the astral plane, using "spirit vision" or another method of mental

travel to access the "Otherworld" or some other direct connection to the "Faerie Realm" (*Gwynedd*). In theory, a Druid could go into the "astral" or "spirit world," make contact with a particular energy stream or spirit, then invite that force consciously back into this "reality." Doing so also actives or increases relationships with elemental beings, strong ties to ancestors and/or other beneficial "*Spirit Guides.*"

A "ward" is a sentient "elementary" spirit ritually created and summoned or conjured "artificially." Often, it is a semi-intelligent force used to guard an area or deflect a certain type of energy. These beings operate as "intentions" based on the polarity and correspondences focused on during their creation. They act as energetic "filters" that "ward away" harmful or unwanted forces and generally occupy the emotional level of existence in likeness to our use of a physical body. As such, the energy composing their existence is not truly "created," but rather "gathered" together and energetically "bound" by spiritual alchemy.

The intention and intensity of need condenses into a manifest or singular "intelligence" that may be named as an "Identity" and sometimes given a "sigil-seal" or "runic glyph"—an energetic "signature" of that name. If it is not given a definitive lifespan, "wards" may take on their own conscious "Identity" as an uncontrolled spirit. If not kept alive energetically with "red meat" offerings—or similar—they may begin to automatically "feed" on the specific type of energy that they are meant to deflect, creating energetic imbalance or resonant distortions in the "physical realm."

Spiritual apparitions seem to occur most often in "smoke" and "fire"—possibly due to an affinity between the fire element and the "spiritual" level of existence. We often also see visions in pools of water and mirrors meaning that the water element carries an affinity with the "Otherworld"—and consequently we find many references in lore to pools, lakes and waterfalls serving as "portals" to the "Otherworld." Even if not distinctly "personi-fied," an elemental spirit and its energy are present in all physical manifestations aligned with that ele-ment.

Alchemical creation of elementary intelligence is easiest if one has a physical representation of the energy to focus on—such as a "figure-statue" or "image." Living parameters of an elementary spirit should always be restricted to a physical object—a ring or stone, &tc.—where the energy is condens-ing and residing when not out performing its tasks. Elementaries and wards should be given simple and specific instructions along with a time limit. They are directed to return to the physical object upon completion of the task—or when a certain amount of time has lapsed—even if the task is in complete.

All animal life is linked with the "Green World" of Nature, and all animals—other than humans, which did not actually naturally evolve on the planet—naturally carry harmonic resonance with their ecosystem and establish equilibrium with their environment. For this reason, all animals are potential allies on the Druid Path and all animals have unique lessons we can benefit from understanding. In essence: trees and animals are the real "instructors" of the Ovate grade.

Symbolism of a "power animal," "totem animal" or "familiar" may be interpreted in various ways. It might be an animal that represents where the Druid is at in their present state of life, or perhaps where they aspire to be. An intuitive Druid might be drawn toward certain animals at different stages of their path based on the lessons they need—or are capable—to learn.

To perform "animal magic" or communication, a Druid must create a telepathic link—just as you would to establish an energetic connection with trees for that type of energy work. A key difference between tree and animal work—at least in this instance—is that energetic vibrations of animals will be at a faster rate than with trees, which will really require a human to "slow" their mind in order to understand properly. Minds of animals and their auric frequency are more easily matched by the natural state of the human condition. One method is to tap into—activate or envision—your own auric energy field and that of the animal (or tree) you are working with, and then link them. To have a proper flow—or circuit of energy—you will have to adjust your "frequency" to match the life-force you are seeking to connect with.

There are some modern practitioners that take this suggestion a step farther—linking up energy centers in their body to the animal's. These are the same that some call "*chakras*" in Eastern traditions, or "*calen*" in Pheryllt Druidry. These "light centers" in the body generate the "auric field" that surrounds the body as well as the polarized—or colored band—frequency that the body is emitting and receiving.

Spirit work involves a strong integration of energies for the duration of a ritual or meditation—and this type of link is only meant to be maintained for relatively short periods of time; like the energetic bond formed in a sexual encounter. It is also important that a Druid separates the "auric link" when the working is completed. The interconnection with all life in the universe is already there—already existent—but to maintain these many strong "cords" consciously while still operating daily life can be very taxing and energetically draining if not maintained properly.

Druids are classically attributed, throughout legend and lore, with the unique ability to "charm" animal-life—to share a kinship with the most innocent forms of natural creation. The material methods of "breaking" an animal are more in line with human society and how humans exchange with each other—whereas in the natural world, life operates based on "will" and the direction of "will-power." Very often we associate the idea of "will-power" and "willingness" with "cooperation." In many instances, similar practices of energetic "personal magnetism" that we employ with humans may be inferred for use with animal-life—depending on the intelligence level of the creature...and most have a higher intelligence than humans would prefer to give credit for. Maintaining spiritual link is helpful in all energy experiments with animals—other suggestions include maintaining physical eye contact as well, the use of soothing gestures and low volume vocalization.

IN THE HENGE OF DRUIDS
—STONE CIRCLES—

In Druid lore, a "henge" is a "suspended" or "hanging" circle —or nemeton—typically constructed of stone, although several ancient remains of wooden examples still exist. Many of the larger sites are "intentionally" designed, sometimes built on a "ley line" or to divert a conjunction of several such "magnetic lines" of force that stretch across the surface of the Earth.

Perhaps the most famous example—Stonehenge—still exists to some degree on the Salisbury Plains in modern-day England. It is sometimes referred to as "Britain's National Temple," and deriving its more popular name from Old English, "*stonheng*," meaning "hanging stones." There are many "megalithic sites" existent throughout Western Europe —and elsewhere throughout the globe—uniquely significant to Druidic tradition. Some esoteric rules still survive in the Bardic lore retained by the Library of Raglan Castle as translated by Meryg Davydd:—

> "It is an institutional usage to form a conventional circle of stones, on the summit of some conspicuous ground, so as to inclose any requisite area of greensward; the stones being so placed as to allow suffici-

ent space for a man to stand between each two of them; except that the two stones of the circle, which most directly confront the eastern sun, should be sufficiently apart to allow at least ample space for three men between them; thus affording an easy ingress to the circle.

"This larger space is called the entrance, or portal; in front of which, at the distance either of three fathoms, or of three times three fathoms, a stone, called station stone, should be so placed as to indicate the eastern cardinal point; to the north of which another stone should be placed, so as to face the eye of the rising sun at the longest summer's day; and to the south of it, an additional one, pointing to the position of the rising sun at the shortest winter's day. These three are called station stones; but, in the centre of the circle, a stone larger than the others should be so placed, that diverging lines, drawn from its middle to the three station stones, may point, severally and directly, to the three particular positions of the rising sun, which they indicate.

"The stones of the circle are called sacred stones, and stones of testimony (*crair*); and the centre stone is variously called the stone of presidency, the altar (*crair*) of gorsedd, the stone of compact (*hog*), and

> the stone of perfection (*armerth*). The whole circle, formed as described, is called the greensward enclosing circle (*cylch ambawr*), the circle of presidency, and the circle of sacred refuge (*gwyngil*); but it is called *trwn* (circle) in some countries. The bards assemble in convention within this circle; and it accords neither with usage nor decency for any other person to enter it, unless desired to do so by a bard."

Stonehenge, however, still remains the most iconic "Druidic Temple"—spiting any controversy over the identity of its builders. The "blue stones" used for its construction originated from a quarry over 150 miles from its present location and according to classical history—a group archaeologists call the "beaker people" brought the stones down from what was then called the Prescelly Mountains of Wales. The name of this range has since changed to the Cambrian Mountains, stretching from the Vale of Glamorgan—the birthplace of the Barddas book—and extending up to the highest peak in the north, near the Isle of Anglesey—an island famous in ancient lore as home to one of the finest "Druid Colleges."

According to lore from the Welsh Pheryllt-Dragon tradition of Druidry, these mountains were once a sanctuary for the proto-Druidic pre-Milesian race, that arrived from Mesopotamia slightly ahead of the developing *La Tene* proto-Celtic culture. It is then quite likely, given our moden misinterpreted timescale of the Irish "Book of Invasions," that the Pheryllt-Dragon Kings are related to the Tuatha d'Anu, who "invaded" Ireland from Wales; not Iberia-Spain.

The outer ring of Stonehenge is 108 feet (40 MY) in diameter and originally composed of 30 vertical standing stones topped by a ring of 30 horizontal lintel stones, each connecting a pair of standing stones—in essence, creating the appearance of a series of doors or portals, 30 in all, each representing an arc of 12 degrees. Another circle—also of 30 standing stones—exists within the larger ring, nearly 9 feet away, approximately 31 MY in diameter. Then, 12 feet from this ring, there is a horse-shoe arrangement, extending from the southeast clockwise to the northwest, of five massive "*trilithons*"—each an individual set of two standing stones topped by a lintel. This also leaves the northeast quadrant open for processional access during ceremonial gatherings and puts the more elaborate "portals" in the "celestial horizon" line of view—the field of the sky where we tend to see the sun and planets. These trilithon "sets" are not connected to each other—such as you find with the outer ring. Within the "horse-shoe" of trilithons is an additional arrangement of 15 smaller solitary standing stones—three "in front" of each trilithon (if looking from the center of the site).

Over the past centuries of revival interest, many scholars have put forth their research and theories regarding Stonehenge and other nearby megalithic sites once held "sacred" by the ancient Druids. Nearly all accounts share one common feature— these sites involve Astronomy, just as we see in the ancient Near East. In 1846, Edward Duke prepared a report summarizing his research for the "Archae- ological Institute of Britain & Ireland," where he states:

> "Astronomy was the earliest of all sci- ences, and was the first which brought into exercise the faculties of the mind of man. It probably originated in Chaldaea, and traveled from Babylon in succession to Egypt, Greece, and Rome, and from thence descended to modern times and spread it- self throughout all nations. The sciences travel faster than the arts, they may be communicated orally to the many at once, but the knowledge of the arts is transfer- able alone from man to man.

> "The Ancient Druids developed a complex series of temples forming a magnificent planetarium—on the face of the land, they formed so vast a stationary *orrery*, con- structed on a meridional line of 32 miles in length. The conception was as sublime as its execution was wonderful! It cannot be

denied that these worshipers of the planets, were imbued with an intimate knowledge of science of Astronomy."

[More information from this article may be found in *"Draconomicon-2: The Pheryllt Researches."*]

ThE DRUID SACRAMENTAL
—RITUAL LITURGY—

The liturgy for the "Druid Sacramental" was developed in the mid-1990's for "Merlyn Stone's Book of Shadows" (prior to a release of the "Sorcerer's Handbook") used by two small Druid groups in Denver, Colorado—"Draconic Celtic Lodge of Druids" (DCLOD) and the "Elven Fellowship Circle of Magick" (EFCOM).

THE EIGHT GROVE FESTIVALS

a.) Winter Solstice: Rebirth of the Sun King
   (*Dec. 21-22*)

b.) Imbolc: Festival of Light (*Feb. 1*)

c.) Spring Equinox: Festival of Life
   (*March 21-22*)

d.) Beltane: Festival of Flowers and Fire (*May 1*)

e.) Summer Solstice: Festival of Oaks and Stones
   (*June 21-22*)

f.) Lughnassadh: Marriage of Lugh (Aug. 1)

g.) Autumn Equinox: Harvest Festival
   (*Sept. 21-22*)

h.) Samhain: Festival of Ancestors and Spirits
   (*Oct. 31-Nov. 1*)

Since so few authentic ritual scripts and ancient suggestions appear for modern neodruid practitioners, this type of layout—or something similar—is popularly executed by contemporary Orders and groups. The liturgy text provided here is both applicable to solitary practitioners and groups. Its ceremonial formula is divided among the eight "Grove Festivals" observed each year.

The neopagan "Wheel of the Year" is one of the more authentic revival efforts conducted by neodruids. Gorsedd Druids or "Initiates of the Third Circle" are responsible for leading and executing all primary solar public festival ceremonies.

1.
Formation of the "Circle of Stones" or *nemeton*.

2.
Lighting the ceremonial incense:

> 1-part *mistletoe* and 1-part *oak leaf*.

3.
Light a white candle in the center of your workspace and say:

> *Here I stand on the threshold between worlds, at a time that is not a time, in a place that is not a place, on a day that is not a day. Yet I am here to occupy this sacred nemeton, to be at one with the many gods, who are but faces of the One and True God. I claim for the moment outside*

of time and space, to attain the right of Godhood for myself.

4.

Consecration of the Circle and ritual implements. Hold your hands over a cup/bowl of water and a plate of salt, and say:

I ask the water spirits to come and bless this water. I ask the earth spirits to come and bless this salt. Water and earth are manifest here, blessed, and contained before me.

Dip the magical items into the salt, then the water (or sprinkle water on something if necessary) and say:

Blessed are these elements and all that makes contact with them. Almighty are the Elder Gods, the ancient, eternal, and ever-shinning Masters.

Drop the salt from the plate into the container of water, and say:

Blessed is the alchemical change. Elements unite. Energies swirl. Fusion and transformation creates.

Walk clockwise around the inside perimeter of the nemeton (beginning in the east, or perhaps north) and sprinkle the alchemical mixture. When you have returned to the east (or place of beginning), say:

> This sacred nemeton, the Holy Mandala, is sealed, protected, and blessed by the forces of earth and water.

Return to your workspace and hold your hands over the incense and burner. This is not the same as the incense from Step 2, and may be selected as the occasion demands, say:

> I ask the air spirits come and bless this incense. I ask the fire spirits to come and bless this burner.

Light the incense in the burner—charcoal, stick, cone, resin incense, &tc.—and pass the ritual implements (objects) to be blessed through the sacred smoke, and say:

> Blessed are the elements of air and fire, and all that makes contact with them. Almighty are the Elder Gods, the ancient, eternal, and ever-shinning Masters.

Walk clockwise around the boundary of the circle as before, this time with the burning incense, which consecrates and purifies the energies of the sacred space. Say:

> This sacred nemeton, the Holy Mandala, is sealed, purified, and blessed by the forces

of air and fire.

5.

Calling the Inspiration of Awen. See the "Three Rays" of light descending down upon you from above. One is silver; one is crystalline white; and the last is gold. Hold this image for thirty heart-beats (seconds), then speak:

> *Today (tonight) I call upon the strength of the heavens: light of sun, radiance of moon, splendor of fire, speed of lightning, swiftness of wind, depth of sea, stability of earth, firmness of stone. I call upon the clear and omnipresent light.*

6.

The Call to to the Elementals. Say:

> *I do now invite all helpful and friendly energies of other realms to witness and defend this circle, and to aid in the magic performed here. I stand between the gates of realization and manifestation. Perceptual doors to the elemental kingdoms open wide by the sound of my voice. May the Great Universal Spirit be within the hearts of all.*

7.

The Eastern Ward. Go to the east and see an equal-armed yellow cross hanging in the air before you —or you can visualize yourself tracing these archetypal symbols—representing the four winds. As you speak the following, you see a faerie sylph come up to the edge of your circle:

> *Let there be peace in the east. Let the winds of the east blow in perfect harmony with all of Creation. By these words of the east: Gorias, Esras, Paraldas, Powers of Air, Kingdom of Wind, I do summon your infinite powers. Come forth from the east that you will be known. You are welcomed.*

8.
The Southern Ward. Go to the south and see a triangle of flame burning before you, suspended in the air. As you speak the following, you see a dragon emerge and come forth to the nemeton:

> *Let there be peace in the south. Let the flames of the south burn in perfect harmony with all of Creation. By these words of the south: Finias, Uscias, Djinas, Powers of Fire, Kingdom of Flame, I do summon your infinite powers. Open now to me and reveal thy mysteries. Come anger of fire. Come fire of oak. Come oak of knowledge. Come now forth from the south. Come flaming sword of song. Come song of razor edge. You are here welcomed.*

9.

The Western Ward. Go to the west and see your perception of the Holy Grail suspended before you. Take and drink from the cup of life, feeling the soothing energy wash over you. Speak the following and see a beautiful sea-nymph come to the nemeton:

> Let peace rule in the west. Let the tides of the western seas flow in perfect harmony with all of creation. By these words of the west: Murias, Semias, Niksas, Powers of Water, Kingdom of Sea, I do summon your infinite powers. Sea full of fish. fish swarming up. Fertile land. Under-wave bird. Wise salmon. Come forth from the west that you can be known. You are welcomed.

10.

The Northern Ward. Go to the north and see a megalithic trilithon portal before you—two standing stones with a lintel topping them both. As you speak the following, you see an elf emerge from between the two stones and move toward the nemeton:

> Let there be peace in the north. May the trees and stones, grow and rest in perfect harmony with all of Creation. By these words of the Northern Portal: Falias, Mor-

fessas, Ghobas, Spirit of the Land, I invoke
you and call you in. Powers of Earth,
Kingdom of Stone, be here now. Spirit of
the trees, vibrations of the stone, from the
north you are called to this magick circle.
You are welcomed.

11.

Benediction. Return to the centre of your workspace, lower your palms (faced down), and say:

Nid Dim on Duw. Nid Duw ond Dim.
Y Gwir yn Erbyn Byd.
The Truth Against the World.

12.

Light intention-based candles as you verbalize the
purpose of the ceremony (e.g. "I am here..."). The
following are suggested colour combinations for
the "Grove Festivals."

GROVE FESTIVAL—CANDLES

a.) Winter Solstce: 1 green, 1 red, 1
        white.
b.) Imbolc: 2 white, 1 green.
c.) Spring Equinox: 2 green, 1
        white.
d.) Beltane: 2 white, 1 red.

---

e.) Summer Solstice: 1 red, 1
   white, 1 yellow.
f.) Lughnassadh: 1 red, 1 yellow, 1
   green.
g.) Autumn Equinox: 1 red, 1
   white, 1 black.
h.) Samhain: 2 black, 1 white.

13.

Calling the Higher Divine Powers of Creation and
the Archetypes. You may wish to, but need not,
further familiarize with the Celtic Mythos so that
you can better envision deity forms at your festivals. [If you feel the need, you could even
substitute a different pantheon.] Then Say:

*Awen, Memw, Akasha, IAO (ee-ah-oh),
Pharon. Powers of the Earth, rising up
from the stone, wind, flame and sea, en-
circle and empower me. Strengthen my
aura. Archetypes of the festival, you are
here honored, as you have been for thousands of years. You do I call forth on this
day (night) to join this sacred ceremony.*

GROVE FESTIVAL— DEITIES

a.) Winter Solstice: Kernunnos,
   Mabon.
b.) Imbolc: D'Anu, Brighid.

c.) Spring Equinox: Taliesen,
   Epona.
d.) Beltane: Bel, Blodduwedd.
e.) Summer Solstice: Arianrhod,
   Oghma.
f.) Lughnassadh: Lugh, D'Anu.
g.) Autumn Equinox: Bran,
   Branwen.
h.) Samhain: Gwyn ap Nudd,
   Samhan.

14.

The Summoning/Conjuring. Say:

Moon, stars, mist, and sun: By the powers above, my will be done. Earth, air, water, and fire: I summon forth what I desire. Oak, ash, thorn, and vine, conjured here are powers Divine. Dragons deep and faeries bold: As above, so below.

15.

Blessing of the Grove. Say:

I come forth to bare witness to the strength and unity of the Grove, where rests this sacred nemeton, the Holy Mandala. Between the roots and branches of the sacred trees, I standfast. I possess the strength of Oak with deep roots and reaching branch-

es. Blessed is the earth. Blessed is the Grove. Blessed be the All.

16.
The Festival Incantation. If the liturgy is used for another purpose, that ritual working would be performed here.

a.)
Winter Solstice: *Farewell to the Dark Lord. All gather and witness the rebirth of the Sun King. Hail to the Sun King who is reborn. Spirits of the Yule-log and the candles thereon, bring to us all good health and cheer. Divine child of light, rejoice in thy existence.*

b.)
Imbolc: *Rekindle the flame. Clear out the old in the house and heart. Enter the new. Shedding skin. Purification. Infinite possibilities uniting to manifest. Earth's slumber soon comes to the end. Great Earth dreaming, remember me.*

c.)
Spring Equinox: *Now I plant the seed of new beginnings. I ask the Forces of Nature to allow it to grow in the time of new growth. Good tidings and welcome, awakening Earth. Equality. The balance of power.*

Renewal. Warmth and love are strengthening the heart of Creation. The Darkness has been dispelled.

d.)

Beltane: *The Earth has now come alive to breed and multiply. Fertility and growth bring maturity. Ah, the Fires of Bel. Oh, the May Queen of Flowers. Look, the Rainbow Children. See, the May Poll. The Cauldron of Inspiration and fertility is overturned, pouring forth blessings upon all of Creation.*

e.)

Summer Solstice: *We gather at the nemeton to celebrate life and the maturity of life. This day marks the annual peak of the Sun King's potency. Yours is the life-giving force, burning within the heart and soul of every being in Creation. Burn deeply within my spirit. Might Sun King, yours is the power that burns and blesses. I stand to give vigil to thy power. Make me a vessel of sacred fire.*

f.)

Lughnassadh: *Lord of the wheat and the corn, bless me now as I come upon the harvest season. Help me to use the fruits of the seed that was planted and has matur-*

ed. *Change comes. The darkness is drawing ever near. I reap the sown seed as I prepare for a time of great hibernation. Now comes a time of looking inward. Bless the first harvest, that it may sustain me through the dark months.*

g.)

Autumn Equinox: *From life to death, I am renewed. The face of the Earth is ready for renewal. Now comes the second harvest. My lord and lady of the shadows gain reign. Maintain and protect me, my home, and my family. May the harvest of my efforts be plentiful for the coming winter. I watch and wait in silence as the darkness draws near.*

h.)

Samhain: *Death comes upon us in full circle. The veil is lowered between this world and the next. Now, I do reap the third and final harvest. The shadow of the dark goddess falls upon the land, spreading out frozen waters of ending and new life. Here do I call my ancestral spirits and the shades of the ancient Druids and Masters, to join me in this sacred festival. We feast to good health and happiness. May both health and happiness be in abundance, now and forever more.*

17.

Ceremonial Feast and retelling of Celtic/Bardic Tales—also see the Bardic Tradition Eisteddfodd addendum given below.

18.

Dismissal and Thanks to Archeypes and Deities called.

19.

Dismissal and Thanks to the Faeries, Nature Spirits, Elemental, and Directional Wards called.

20.

Extinguishing the Energies of the Active Nemeton.

—EISTEDDFODD ADDENDUM—

This rite can be used by any number of participants and may be amended for any type of group work or "circle magic." The ceremonial observation is most effective in a "circle" of trees and/or stones. Once the participants are prepared, procession to the northeast corner of the Nemeton bringing all tools and items with you and begin.

I. OPENING BENEDICTION

<u>Druid King or Arch Druid</u>: *May the Source of All Being and Creation grant us favor and protection; and in protection, strength; and in strength, peace;*

and in peace, understanding; and in understanding comes the True Knowledge of the 'Right Way'; and in the grace of this knowledge may we be granted the will to use it; and in that will, the wisdom to temper the use of knowledge; and in temperance comes mercy; and thru mercy, love; and in love we find the Source of All Being and Creation.

<u>Druid Queen or High Priestess</u>: *The recursive spiral path passes through Annwn ('ah-noon') and returns to the love and favor of the Source. Blessed be the All.*

<u>All</u>: Blessed be the Universe.

II. GRAND INVOCATION

<u>Druid King or Arch Druid</u>: *To bathe in the aethyr of new light and life that swirls about the galaxy. To cleanse away iniquity and mortality so we may join in the harmony of all living beings. Here we stand, beneath the Oaks, beneath the Stones, coming to the place we watched our ancestors go to commune with the Spirit of the Universe.*

<u>Druid Queen or High Priestess</u>: *The stars shine brightly upon this meeting of our people. The Divine Star shines brightly on us now at the hour of our meeting.*

III. ELEMENTAL BENEDICTION

<u>Druid Queen/High Priestess</u>: *Let peace ring out through the four quadrants of the Universe. Within our being may we find peace at the center. In the Secret Grove we meet to share peace. Then, as we go about the lives we lead on the 'Surface World,' we radiate the currents of love and peace and attract the same.*

<u>Druid King/Arch Druid</u>: *Here we stand strong, coming together in answer to the call of our inner vow as Guardians and Keepers of the Earth. Here we stand, side-by-side, heart-to-heart and* [the circle joins hands] *hand-in-hand.* [Release hands.]

<u>Northern Druid Guard</u>: *Guardian of the North, realm and spirits of the Earth Element, 'nature spirits,' Gnomes, Kobold and Drwyds of Falias, hail and welcome to this Nemeton. Extend the currents of peace and stability.*

<u>Eastern Druid Guard</u>: *Guardian of the East, realm and spirits of the Air Element, Ancient and Shinning Ones, Elves and Drwyds of Gorias, hail and welcome to this Nemeton. Extend the currents that enable enlightenment.*

<u>Southern Druid Guard</u>: *Guardian of the South, realm and spirits of Fire, Dragon Priests, fiery sprytes, pict-sidhe and Drwyds of Finias, hail and welcome to this Nemeton. Extend the necessary*

energy for strengthening the will.

<u>Western Druid Guard</u>: *Guardian of the West, realm and spirits of the Water Element, ancestral spirits, merfolk, Drwyds of the past and the Otherworld city of Murias, hail and welcome to this Nemeton. Extend the currents of personal well-being and those that enable the insight of wisdom.*

IV. BARDIC VERSE & STORY

Traditionally, a gathering of Bardic Druids will recite lore and legend at ceremonial gatherings and festival celebrations to preserve such stories. Bardic Traditions call this type of gathing an "*Eisteddfodd*" in the Gaelic-Welsh language, an ancient ceremonial tradition of processions, candle-lighting, stories and "sermons" that were shared. Equivalent to *Step-17* in the reformed liturgy previously given.

V. FESTIVAL OBSERVATIONS

Perform ceremonial celebration or other operations the group has come together to accomplish.

VI. THANKING & DISMISSING ELEMENTAL SPIRITS

<u>Druid King or Arch Druid</u>: *May the Source of All Being and Creation grant us favor and protection; and in protection, strength; and in strength, peace;*

and in peace, understanding; and in understanding comes the True Knowledge of the 'Right Way'; and in the grace of this knowledge may we be granted the will to use it; and in that will, the wisdom to temper the use of knowledge; and in temperance comes mercy; and thru mercy, love; and in love we find the Source of All Being and Creation.

<u>Druid Queen or High Priestess</u>: *Let peace ring out through the four quadrants of the Universe. Within our being may we find peace at the center. In the Secret Grove we meet to share peace. Then, as we go about the lives we lead on the 'Surface World,' we radiate the currents of love and peace and attract the same.*

<u>Western Druid Guard</u>: *Guardian of the West, spirit of the Wave and realm of Sea, we thank thee for thy attendance this day/eve as you witness and remember the ceremony we practice in memory of the rites of our ancestors. May you return again when hence we call. Hail and Farewell. Go in peace.*

<u>Southern Druid Guard</u>: *Guardian of the South, spirit of the Flame and realm of Fire, we thank thee for thy attendance this day/eve as you witness and remember the ceremony we practice in memory of the rites of our ancestors. May you return again when hence we call. Hail and Farewell.*

Go in peace.

Eastern Druid Guard: *Guardian of the East, spirit of the Wind and realm of Air, we thank thee for thy attendance this day/eve as you witness and remember the ceremony we practice in memory of the rites of our ancestors. May you return again when hence we call. Hail and Farewell. Go in peace.*

Northern Druid Guard: *Guardian of the North, spirits of Stone and Wood and realm of Earth, we thank thee for thy attendance this day/eve as you witness and remember the ceremony we practice in memory of the rites of our ancestors. May you return again when hence we call. Hail and Farewell. Go in peace.*

VII. CLOSING BENEDICTION

Druid King/Arch Druid: *Before departing from this place, we release the field surrounding this sacred nemeton, grounding the energy of Earth, releasing to the Sky the energies of Air, pushing down the currents of Fire deep into the 'Core of Gaea' and pouring the Waters back into the Sea. So mote it be.*

Druid Queen/High Priestess: *As we have come in peace, so do we leave in peace. We are the 'Children of the Stars,' beings of light, life and love. In departing, we project and radiate peaceful energy* *and positive power throughout the Universe, dispersing the energies of light and truth gathered here this day/night. Blessed Be.*

<u>All</u>: *Blessed Be.*

<u>Druid King/Arch Druid</u>: *Y Gwir Yn Erbyn Byd.*

<u>All</u>: *The Truth Against The World.*

<u>Druid Queen/High Priestess</u>: *May our circle now stand open, though it is still a circle and never broken. The power of the 'Magick Sphere' of the is 'Gorsedd/Grove of [group name]' ever lives here.*

<u>All</u>: *Awen* ["*ah-oo-een*"]

—GREAT TREE RITE ADDENDUM—

Lunar orientation of the "Great Tree Rite" compliments solar orientation of the original "Druid Sacramental" solar liturgy—which is most applicable to seasonal observances. Here in the Great Tree Rite, we see potential application to the lunar cycle—observation of the full or new moon. It is further possible that many traditional solar rites were performed during the day, leaving nighttime as the domain of lunar rites. This ritual text continues the same "elemental alignment" as the former rites and may be adapted to either group or solitary practice. Performance of the "Great Tree Rite" begins with the first eleven steps given in the original "Druid Sacramental" liturgy formula. Intentions of the rite are proclaimed and then the operator(s) continue with the remainder of this ritual text.

<u>Leader</u>: *We are here to give witness to the unity and strength of the magic circle, this mandala of love most holy. We, the Druids, the Children of Light, are at one with thee, O Sacred Tree. You, who stands as an eternal symbol of the Circle of Light and Life. You, who represent our eternal link with the ever-present Source. We honor and imitate you as the perfect living specimen of the Source of All Being and Creation. We watch you as you progress through the sacred Earth Year.*

<u>North</u>: *The beginnings, middles, and ends of the sacred Earth Year.*

<u>East</u>: *The balance and equinox forces of the sacred Earth Year.*

<u>South</u>: *Tonight (today) we coven together, man and tree, acknowledging the Sacred Grove.*

<u>West</u>: *We celebrate the strength, love, and unity of the Sacred Grove, and in that celebration we honor the central icon of its existence: The Great Tree.*

<u>East</u>: *From the Eastern Winds we are granted a season of growth, as the sun emerges in the spring.*

South: *From the Southern Flame we are granted a season of fullness, as the sun warms the summer.*

West: *From the Western Waves we are granted a season of transformation with the shifting tides of autumn.*

North: *From the Firmness of Northern Ground we are granted a season of stability, self-reflection, and stillness, as the Earth hibernates and is renewed through winter.*

Leader: *The calendrical month ___, the Oghamic month of the ___ tree in the ancient Druid's calender.* [Traces the Oghamic rune in the air.] *May the blessing of ___, and the corresponding energies of ___ be projected forth into our auric light.*

GREAT TREE RITE—OGHAM KEYS

January: Alder Tree, *Fearn*, protection and power.

February: Willow Tree, *Saille*, healing and enchantment.

March: Ash Tree, *Nuin*, protection and peace.

April: Hawthorn Tree, *Huatha*, love and purity.

May: Oak Tree, *Duir*, strength and leadership.

June: Holly, *Tinne*, purification and
balance.
July: Hazel Tree, *Coll*, intuition and
creativity.
August: Vine, *Muin*, meditation and
prophecy.
September: Ivy, *Gort*, protection and
growth.
October: Reed, *Ngetal*, intense energy and
direct action.
13th:* Elder Tree, *Ruis*, completion and
reflection.
November: Birth Tree, *Beith*, fertility and
growth.
December: Rowan Tree, *Luis*, strength
and insight.

East: *May the Sacred Grove and the Great Tree grant us the strength of the ancient Druids.*

South: *We hereby swear (reaffirm) our Guardianship of Gaea, the Sacred Grove, the Great Tree, and all life in Creation.*

West: *May the gentle rains bless all of Creation, nurturing and giving life, forever and always.*

---

* *"13th Month"*—A *"Blue Moon"* or Samhain
(*Oct.31-Nov.2*) or else some other *"New Years"*
period to synchronize the luni-solar calendar.

Leader: *The entangled roots of the Great Tree shall live deep within our being, offering nourishment and stability to all of its faithful guardians.*

North: *And in between the roots and branches, we stand as the Guardians, the Keepers of the Earth, we who live in imitation of Oak Trees.*

East: *Our branches reach into the same sky proving that ascension is the purpose and goal of all life.*

South: *Great Universal Spirit, beings inhabiting this Sacred Tree, we stand here as your worthy guardians, and Keepers of the Earth and her mysteries.*

West: *May we grow to become our full potential from the seedlings we now are. May seeds plant in the world, bloom and flourish, spreading the true beauty and love of the Source of All, shared by all those receptive.*

Leader: [Traces Ogham sign on the tree; then knocks three times lightly on the trunk, intoning the name of the tree, perhaps in Celtic language, with each knock.] *O Great Tree, you are hereby awakened by the Druids of the ancient and ineffable knowledge.*

North: *May the ground that covers the roots, forever and always be blessed with all that is good and holy. May all of creation grow as the trees in* *the forest, each beautiful in their own uniqueness, yet still sharing the same Earth in which too spread roots and call home.*

<u>Leader</u>: *We are united in our strengths, our faith, our love, and our trust. Ours in the bond that must endure all other bonds. The Truth Against the World.*

<u>All</u>: *The Truth Against The World.*

<u>Leader</u>: *Through True Knowledge, Power.*

<u>All</u>: *Through True Knowledge, Power.*

<u>Leader</u>: *So mote it be.*

THE ORIGINAL HARDCOVER 2-VOLUME SET

SUMERIAN RELIGION

*Introducing the Anunnaki Gods
of Mesopotamian Neopaganism*

Mardukite Liber-50

by Joshua Free

BABYLONIAN MYTH & MAGIC

*Spiritual Traditions and Mysticism
in Mesopotamian Anunnaki Religion*

Mardukite Liber-51+E

by Joshua Free

SYSTEMOLOGY BASICS HARDCOVER SET

THE POWER OF ZU

*Applying Mardukite Zuism and
Systemology to Everyday Life
Systemology Liber-S1-Z*
based on a lecture series
by Joshua Free

THE WAY INTO THE FUTURE

*A Handbook for the New Human
Systemology Liber-S1-W*
collected works mini-anthology
by Joshua Free

The Pathway to Self-Honesty

GO FURTHER AND BE

CRYSTAL CLEAR

CRYSTAL CLEAR

(*Handbook for Seekers*)

Mardukite Systemology Liber-2B
by Joshua Free

Take control of your destiny
and chart the first steps
toward your own spiritual evolution.
Realize new potentials of the
Human Condition with
a Self-guiding handbook for
Self-Processing toward
Self-Actualization
in Self-Honesty using actual
techniques and training
provided for the coveted
"Mardukite Systemology Grade-III
Self-Defragmentation Course Program"
—once only available
directly and privately from
the underground Systemology Society.

Discover the amazing power behind the
applied spiritual technology
used for counseling and advisement in
the tradition of Mardukite Zuism.

JOSHUA FREE

PUBLISHED BY THE **JOSHUA FREE** IMPRINT REPRESENTING

The Founding Church of Mardukite Zuism

THE JOSHUA FREE IMPRINT
JFI PUBLICATIONS

MARDUKITE
ZUISM

mardukite.com

www.ingramcontent.com/pod-product-compliance
Lightning Source LLC
Chambersburg PA
CBHW011236120626
46549CB00009B/3290